THE BAKERSFIELD SOUND

Buck Owens, Merle Haggard, and California Country

Published on the occasion of the exhibition
The Bakersfield Sound:
Buck Owens, Merle Haggard, and California Country
Country Music Hall of Fame® and Museum
Opening March 2012

With essays by Scott B. Bomar, Randy Poe, and Robert Price
Introduction by Dwight Yoakam

Country Music Foundation Press
Nashville, Tennessee
2012

Country Music Foundation Press
222 Fifth Avenue South
Nashville, Tennessee 37203
(615) 416-2001

This publication was created by the Staff of the Country Music Hall of Fame® and Museum.

Editors: Michael Gray and John W. Rumble

Printer: Lithographics, Inc., Nashville, TN

Except where otherwise credited, images in this book come from the collection of the
Country Music Hall of Fame® and Museum.

Introduction

Since 1967, the Country Music Hall of Fame® and Museum has used many strategies to fulfill its mission of preserving the evolving history of country music and educating its audiences. In addition to museum exhibits, our school and public programs, CD and DVD reissues, Web site, and publications help us reach fans, students, scholars, and members of the music industry, in Nashville and around the world.

In planning this companion book for *The Bakersfield Sound: Buck Owens, Merle Haggard, and California Country*, our museum staff decided to offer readers a publication that would supplement—but not duplicate—the exhibit itself. In these pages, readers will find images of many items featured in the exhibit, along with additional rare treasures saved by Bakersfield veterans and their friends, family members, and business associates.

To provide insight into Bakersfield's many contributions to the music world, we invited several experts to prepare essays. Scott Bomar, a songwriter, researcher, and music industry professional who produced and annotated Bear Family Records' five-CD box set on Bakersfield pioneer Red Simpson, gives an overview of the city's history in "Dim Lights, Thick Smoke, and Loud, Loud Music: The Story of the Bakersfield Sound."

Author and music publishing executive Randy Poe, who is preparing the authorized biography of Buck Owens, shares his extensive knowledge of the singer's career in "From the Back Roads of Texas to the Streets of Bakersfield: The Musical Journey of Buck Owens."

Robert Price, a reporter, columnist, and editor at *The Bakersfield Californian* since 1988, assesses Merle Haggard's impact in "Merle Haggard: His Songs, His Life, His Legacy."

Dwight Yoakam, perhaps the Bakersfield Sound's most ardent champion among younger artists who have drawn upon the city's musical heritage, gives his personal tribute to his musical heroes.

It is our hope that, taken together, these essays and reminiscences—and the images they accompany—provide a revealing picture of an extraordinary place during an extraordinary period of America's musical and cultural history.

—Michael Gray and John W. Rumble

Contributors

Scott B. Bomar is a songwriter, researcher, and music industry professional who grew up in Nashville. After completing his graduate studies at Vanderbilt University, he relocated to Los Angeles, where he has worked with Sony / ATV Music and Universal Music Group. He recently produced and annotated Bear Family Records' five-CD box set chronicling the career of Bakersfield pioneer Red Simpson, and is writing a book about the Bakersfield Sound.

Randy Poe began his music career as a country disc jockey in Haleyville, Alabama. He moved to New York in 1980, becoming executive director of the Songwriters Hall of Fame two years later. Since 1985 he has been the president of Leiber & Stoller Music Publishing. Poe is the author of several books, including *Skydog: The Duane Allman Story* and *Stalking the Red Headed Stranger*. He is working on the authorized biography of Buck Owens.

Robert Price has been a reporter, columnist, and editor at *The Bakersfield Californian* since 1988. His work includes the *Journal of Country Music*'s November 2001 cover-story profile of Dwight Yoakam and the liner notes for Time-Life Records' 2006 Merle Haggard retrospective, *Merle Haggard: The Original Outlaw*. Since 2002 Price has taught courses on Bakersfield's musical history at California State University Bakersfield and Bakersfield Community College.

Dwight Yoakam was born in rural Kentucky, raised in Ohio, and gravitated in 1978 to California, where Buck Owens and Merle Haggard upheld Bakersfield's musical heritage. Yoakam opened shows for L.A. roots-rock acts and soon recorded his own best-selling albums. Fascinated by the Bakersfield Sound, he coaxed Owens out of retirement for their #1 1988 duet recording of "Streets of Bakersfield." Yoakam has maintained his allegiance to Owens and the Bakersfield Sound, as proven by the release in 2007 of *Dwight Sings Buck*, an entire album of songs by his hero.

Dear Museum Friend,

The sounds of Bakersfield, California, reverberate through country music history like a sustained note from a Fender Telecaster guitar. The stripped-down, incisive music created in this oil town, and the great musicians identified with it, have long been part of the American art form documented by the Country Music Hall of Fame® and Museum.

Indeed, our core exhibit, *Sing Me Back Home*, takes its name from a song by Bakersfield legend Merle Haggard, and our record label has issued two albums—*Live at Carnegie Hall* (1988) and *Young Buck: The Complete Pre-Capitol Recordings of Buck Owens* (2001)—by Buck Owens, another Hall of Fame member from Bakersfield. This book and the exhibit it complements honor a creative community whose influence still resonates in the twenty-first century, adding an important chapter to the Museum's mission to collect, preserve, and present country music history in all of its glory and complexity.

Our Museum's exhibits have featured the artifacts of numerous Bakersfield musicians and entrepreneurs, who are also well represented in the Museum's massive Frist Library and Archive. Besides the two albums by Owens, the Museum has compiled and annotated Bakersfield-related historic record reissues on Merle Haggard (the box set *Down Every Road*) and Hall of Famer Jean Shepard (*Honky Tonk Heroine: Classic Capitol Recordings, 1952–1964*). Several Museum-produced books also have analyzed the Bakersfield scene.

Our look at Bakersfield will feature public programs—including interviews, panels, and live performances—further exploring the city's musical history and influence. Many will be streamed live at CountryMusicHallofFame.org, which includes a schedule of all Museum programs.

To tell the story, we went to the people who created it. We are grateful to the folks at Hag, Inc., Buck Owens Productions, and Buck Owens' Crystal Palace for their contributions to this project. Dwight Yoakam was a great help, too. We hope you'll enjoy this walk down the streets of Bakersfield, and we thank you for your interest and support.

Sincerely,

Kyle Young
Director

The Country Music Hall of Fame® and Museum is operated by the Country Music Foundation, Inc., a section 501(c)(3) not-for-profit educational organization chartered by the state of Tennessee in 1964.

222 FIFTH AVENUE SOUTH | NASHVILLE, TENNESSEE 37203 | PHONE 615.416.2001 | FAX 615.255.2245

www.CountryMusicHallofFame.org

Table of Contents

Acknowledgments

This book and the exhibit it complements represent the contributions of many generous individuals and organizations. Rose Waters provided invaluable access and introductions to musicians and others in Bakersfield's extensive orbit. Doug Paisley, Brad Paisley's father, was never too busy to search for Brad's artifacts and photos. Frank Mull welcomed us into the world of Merle Haggard.

Country Music Hall of Fame® and Museum board member Lon Helton put our staff in touch with Buck and Bonnie Owens's son Michael, who played a key role in assembling materials for the exhibit and for this book. Michael and his brother Buddy Alan, along with Mel Owens, Buck's nephew, supplied both artifacts and images. Jim Shaw, of Buck Owens Productions, which includes Buck Owens' Crystal Palace, facilitated the loan of most of the Buck Owens artifacts in the exhibit. Mr. Shaw also supplied numerous photos from the Buck Owens Private Foundation, many of which appear in the exhibit and / or the book.

Marty Stuart was especially helpful in loaning artifacts and other materials, and in helping our museum staff make contacts with other persons vital to this project. We are also grateful to Pete Anderson, Deke Dickerson, Dallas Frazier, Jody Maphis, Rose Lee Maphis, Billy Mize, and Buddy Mize for their assistance. Likewise, our thanks go to Fuzzy Owen, Glenn J. Pogatchnik, Jimmy Sanders, Joe Saunders, Karen Saunders, Red and Joyce Simpson, and Thomas S. Sims. We are grateful to Don Rich's sons Vance and Vic Ulrich, Ray Urquhart, and Richard Weize for their contributions, and to Nancy Kruh for her editorial skills. Capitol / EMI and the Grand Ole Opry Archives supplied photos.

This project reflects the work of many Country Music Hall of Fame® and Museum staff members. Although space prohibits listing them all, the contributions of Vice President, Museum Services Carolyn Tate; Vice President, Museum Programs Jay Orr; exhibit co-curators Mick Buck and Tim Davis; co-curator and editor Michael Gray; editor John W. Rumble; creative director Warren Denney; lead designer Emily Marlow, and designer Brandon Riesgo deserve special mention.

Special thanks go to supporting sponsors the Academy of Country Music, the Ford Motor Company Fund, and SunTrust Bank, as well as Buck Owens' Crystal Palace / Buck Owens Private Foundation. The GAC Television Network and Cumulus Media Inc. / Cumulus Broadcasting Inc. gave additional support. The Tennessee Arts Commission and the Metro Nashville Arts Commission, which provide essential annual operating support for the museum, helped underwrite publications, school programs, and public programs.

Finally, we are deeply indebted to Dwight Yoakam for sharing his passion for—and insights into—Bakersfield's musical heritage, and for contributing his time and talents to make the book and the exhibit a success.

Photos courtesy of
Dwight Yoakam

Survivors' Voices

The musical sound from Bakersfield, California, is undeniably the most infectious and glittering embodiment of jet-aged musical expression to storm forth from the aftermath of hardship that assaulted the United States in the 1930s Dust Bowl. That seminal event led to one of the greatest human migrations in the country's history. From Arkansas, Texas, Oklahoma, and throughout the central plains, hundreds of thousands were driven by brutal and often life-threatening circumstance toward the West Coast, with hopes and dreams for survival of their families in tow. Although material components and elements of those lives had been ripped to pieces as they were sent careening toward an unknown future by the catastrophic events of that decade, the people maintained possession of a central element of cultural identity through their music.

That surviving voice—which in its earliest, migrated manifestations was often little more than a mournful moan or lament about the world and lives that had been destroyed—continued to evolve. It gradually grew to a musical crescendo with the commercial success of recording artists such as Tommy Collins, Wynn Stewart, Buck Owens, and Merle Haggard. Their voices, still carrying the raw-edged echoes of irreverent outcasts, not only demanded the attention of listeners around the world, but would ultimately influence the future of country music and its performers for decades.

—Dwight Yoakam

Greetings from **Bakersfield** California
"Queen of the San Joaquin Valley"

THE BAKERSFIELD SOUND
Buck Owens, Merle Haggard, and California Country

A TOWN CALLED BAKERSFIELD

Bakersfield is located near the southern end of California's fertile San Joaquin Valley. Founded in 1869, the city is the seat of Kern County, one of America's leading producers of cotton, grapes, citrus, almonds, and oil.

Beginning in the 1930s, Kern County's orchards and oilfields lured thousands of workers and their families from the South, Southwest, and Midwest. They had been displaced by the ravages of the Dust Bowl and the Great Depression, or were simply looking for employment. The influx of so many rural southerners and midwesterners helped Bakersfield cultivate a socially conservative climate, out of step with California's progressive image.

Some of these migrants—disparaged as "Okies" by other residents—would become the creators of Bakersfield's best-known export: country music. With its thriving nightclub scene and concentration of exceptional musical talent, the city, with a population of 57,000 in 1960, emerged as the hub of a unique sound that challenged Nashville for chart supremacy.

Map and inset, 1946.

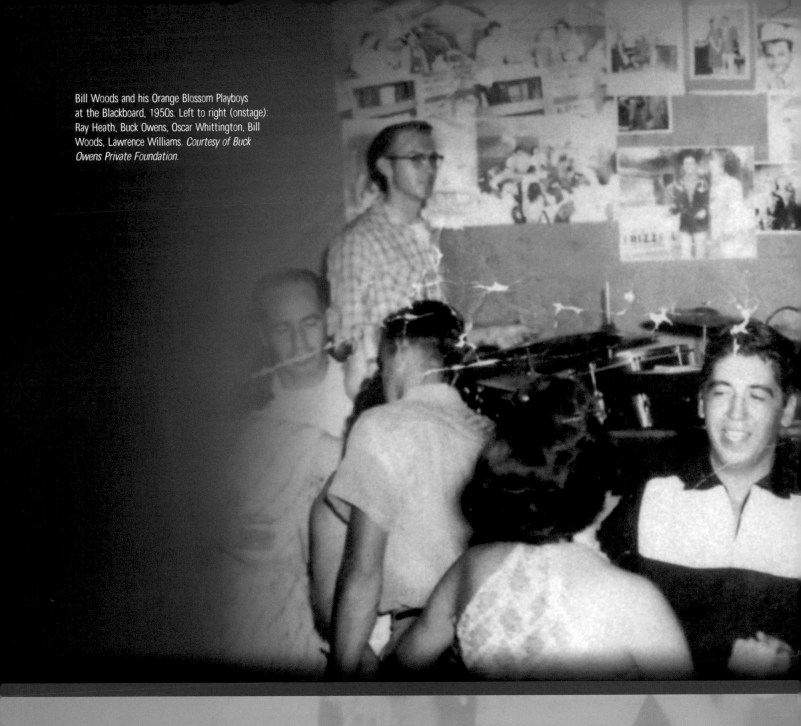

Bill Woods and his Orange Blossom Playboys at the Blackboard, 1950s. Left to right (onstage): Ray Heath, Buck Owens, Oscar Whittington, Bill Woods, Lawrence Williams. *Courtesy of Buck Owens Private Foundation.*

DIM LIGHTS, THICK SMOKE, AND LOUD, LOUD MUSIC

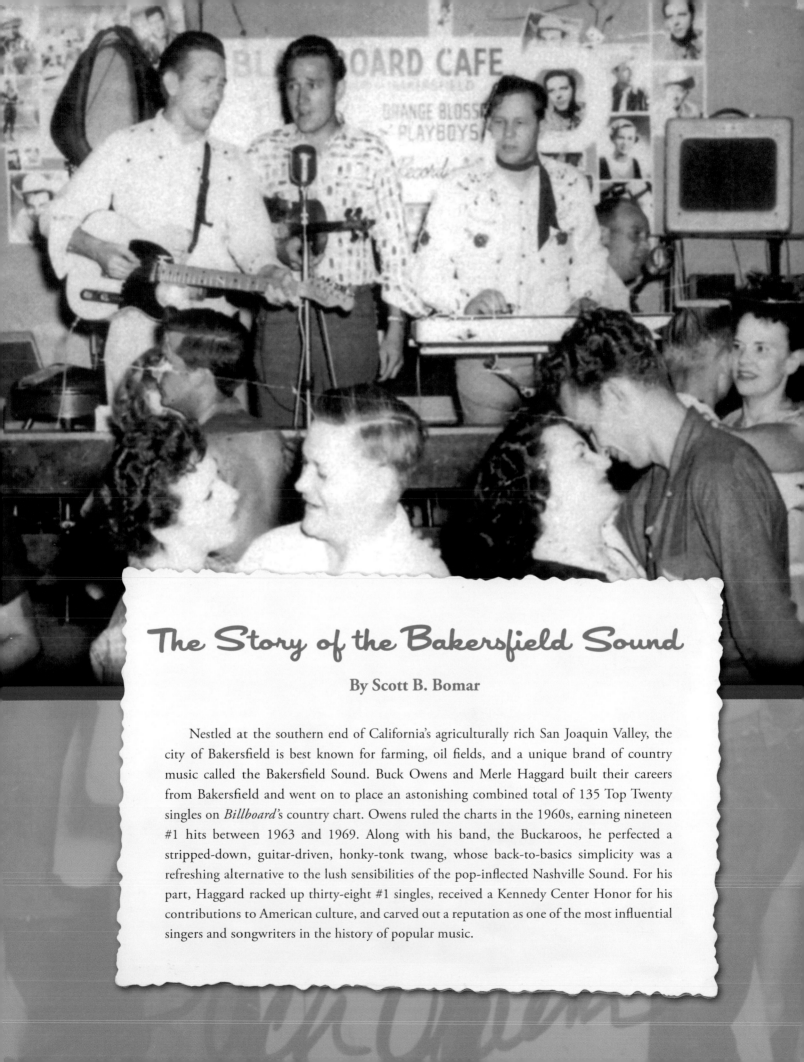

The Story of the Bakersfield Sound

By Scott B. Bomar

Nestled at the southern end of California's agriculturally rich San Joaquin Valley, the city of Bakersfield is best known for farming, oil fields, and a unique brand of country music called the Bakersfield Sound. Buck Owens and Merle Haggard built their careers from Bakersfield and went on to place an astonishing combined total of 135 Top Twenty singles on *Billboard*'s country chart. Owens ruled the charts in the 1960s, earning nineteen #1 hits between 1963 and 1969. Along with his band, the Buckaroos, he perfected a stripped-down, guitar-driven, honky-tonk twang, whose back-to-basics simplicity was a refreshing alternative to the lush sensibilities of the pop-inflected Nashville Sound. For his part, Haggard racked up thirty-eight #1 singles, received a Kennedy Center Honor for his contributions to American culture, and carved out a reputation as one of the most influential singers and songwriters in the history of popular music.

Above: On the set of *Cousin Herb's Trading Post*, c. 1953. Left to right: Herb Henson, Johnny Cuviello, Billy Mize, Jelly Sanders, Bill Woods, Dallas Frazier, Carlton Ellis.

Left: Sheet music for Ferlin Husky and Jean Shepard's recording of "A Dear John Letter."

But the music Owens and Haggard created didn't simply appear fully formed from their respective imaginations. "We represent the end results of all the years of country music in this town," Haggard reflected in 1995. Country luminaries with Bakersfield ties include Bob Wills, who had a weekly gig at Bakersfield's Beardsley Ballroom in the mid-1940s, and legendary songwriter Leon Payne ("Lost Highway," "I Love You Because"), who briefly lived in Bakersfield in that same decade. During the 1950s, Bakersfield's Billy Mize was a fixture on Los Angeles TV shows *Town Hall Party* and Gene Autry's *Melody Ranch*. In addition, Mize recorded for Decca and other labels while writing barroom anthems such as "Who Will Buy the Wine." Ferlin Husky, best known for his later hits "Gone" (1957) and "Wings of a Dove" (1960), was the first Bakersfield artist to record for Hollywood's powerful Capitol Records, signing with the label in 1951. With his help, Husky's roommates and protégés Dallas Frazier and Tommy Collins launched their own successful careers with Capitol. Frazier eventually composed such hits as "Alley Oop," "There Goes My Everything," and "Elvira," while Collins recorded a half-dozen Top Ten records and wrote "If You Ain't Lovin' (You Ain't Livin')," a hit for both Faron Young and George Strait. In the 1960s and '70s Capitol continued to find fertile ground in Bakersfield with releases by artists including Bobby Durham, David Frizzell, and Red Simpson, who penned standards such as "Close Up the Honky Tonks" and achieved several hits with blacktop-themed fare including "I'm a Truck."

The boys, however, weren't the only ones to find success in Bakersfield. Jean Shepard, who was raised seventy-five miles north, in Visalia, topped the country charts in 1953 with "A Dear John Letter," her million-selling crossover duet with Ferlin Husky. It was the first national hit to feature a studio band of Bakersfield musicians. Bonnie Owens came to Bakersfield in the early 1950s. Being the only woman to marry both Buck Owens and Merle Haggard would qualify her as the First Lady of the Bakersfield Sound, but she was also a talented singer, placing four albums in *Billboard*'s country Top Forty.

Other notable female artists who made lasting contributions include Susan Raye, Kay Adams, and Barbara Mandrell. Working with Buck Owens, Raye often appeared on *Hee Haw* and recorded fifteen Top Twenty singles, including 1971's "L.A. International Airport." She began her association with Owens after replacing Adams as the "girl singer" in his touring show. Adams, who had a minor hit with "Little Pink Mack" (1966) and two Top Forty solo country albums, was discovered while singing on Dave Stogner's Bakersfield television program. Stogner's show also featured Red Simpson and Norm Hamlet, who would later become Merle Haggard's longtime steel guitarist. It was Hamlet who first taught a nine-year-old Barbara Mandrell to play the steel. Though she would eventually become a Nashville superstar, Mandrell released her first single, "Queen for a Day," on Bakersfield's Mosrite label in 1966.

Above: Bonnie Owens, First Lady of the Bakersfield Sound. *Courtesy of Michael Owens.*

Right: In the 1990s, Fender presented this re-issue of its 1952 Telecaster to Bill Woods to honor his pioneering contributions to the Bakersfield Sound. The guitar is signed by Merle Haggard, Billy Mize, Buck Owens, and Red Simpson. *Courtesy of Ray Urquhart. Photo by Bob Delevante.*

The Bakersfield Sound

Bakersfield was undoubtedly a country music hotbed, but what, exactly, is the "Bakersfield Sound?" The term is generally used to describe a hard-edged honky-tonk sensibility characterized by sharp, twanging Fender Telecaster guitars, crying pedal steel, and straight-ahead country vocals—a sound that thrived in Bakersfield clubs in the 1950s and '60s. Yet the term itself is misleading. The music emanating from these venues was by no means homogeneous. One need only compare Buck Owens's razor-sharp honky-tonk attack with Merle Haggard's western swing and blues-inflected recordings to recognize that there is no single Bakersfield Sound. The label is best understood as an umbrella term encompassing a number of strains developed by Haggard, Owens, and their West Coast contemporaries.

In addition, as Merle Haggard stressed in 1999, "What became known as the Bakersfield Sound was always bigger than Bakersfield." Wynn Stewart, for example, is routinely cited as one of the sound's earliest pioneers, even though he never lived there. Moreover, most of the hits by artists associated with Bakersfield were actually recorded at Capitol's Hollywood studios. Some commentators use "Bakersfield Sound" to refer not only to a style of music, but also to the specific era of the 1950s and '60s when a rich musical subculture flourished in and around the city.

Bakersfield's Musical Roots

Many observers have erroneously described the Bakersfield Sound as a reaction to the slicker, pop-oriented Nashville Sound, which dominated much of country radio by the mid-1960s. Although Bakersfield's music was indeed an alternative to Nashville's fare, its roots ran much deeper. The Dust Bowl migration of the 1930s, Hollywood's singing cowboys, western swing's popularity during the war years, early strains of rock & roll, the advent of the solid-body electric guitar, and a pervading spirit of artistic independence and musical innovation all helped to shape Bakersfield's thriving music community.

Though fiddle music was reported in the mining camps during California's Gold Rush, and old-time, folk, and hillbilly tunes could be heard over the state's airwaves from the dawn of radio in the 1920s, Bakersfield's musical story properly began during the Dust Bowl era. In the early 1930s, when economic hardship and crippling drought gripped the southern plains, thousands sought refuge in California, where harvest seasons were longer and work opportunities were reported by relatives and friends who'd already moved west. Between 1935 and 1940, more than 70,000 migrants streamed into the San Joaquin Valley, and thousands of families became squatters in unsanitary makeshift camps. As the established citizenry grew increasingly alarmed, migrants were often derided as ignorant and undesirable "Okies." Many suffered discrimination, uncertain work opportunities, and even physical violence fomented by anti-union businessmen.

By 1937 the federal Farm Security Administration (FSA) had set up camps to ensure sanitation, public health, and worker safety. Naturally, the music these migrants brought with them provided comfort at the end of the workday. In the summers of 1940 and '41, Charles Todd and Robert Sonkin traveled to the Valley on behalf of the Library of Congress's Archive of American Folk Song to document the lives of agricultural workers. Most camps, they found, offered weekly talent shows, sing-alongs, song swaps, or dances. "It was just old-time country music," Todd recalled. "I was amazed at the number of good guitar players. Practically everyone we ran into had a guitar stashed away somewhere."

Top: Dallas Frazier and his father, Floyd, in a California cotton field, early 1940s. One of the most successful songwriters in country music, Frazier was born in Oklahoma and began his music career as a child in Bakersfield. *Courtesy of Dallas Frazier.*

Above: Farm Security Administration camps offered migrants opportunities to attend dances and other musical events.

Dancin' Away the Blues

As families were able to save up a little money, they purchased affordable lots on the outskirts of town. Whether due to economic constraints, prejudices, or simply the desire to maintain community, migrants generally settled in neighborhoods like Little Okie or Oildale, just outside Bakersfield. As in the FSA camps, music and dancing remained an important focus in small taverns such as Bateman's Club, Ma Scott's, and the Chicken Coop, which allowed musicians to play for tips. Dancing also continued in large halls like the Barn on Stine Road. This venue offered western music as early as 1936, when the Southern Stars—then including future western swing great Spade Cooley—were the house band.

Dance halls proliferated in the 1940s as the expanding economy put money in the pockets of day laborers, oil field workers, and fruit pickers. In 1946, Bob Wills, the patron saint of western swing and a hero to nearly everyone in Bakersfield's country music colony, appeared weekly at Beardsley Ballroom, then the most popular spot in town. "I got up one night and slipped out the window of our house when I was about eleven years old," Merle Haggard remembered, "and rode my bike to Beardsley Ballroom to try to go see Bob Wills. . . . You know what I learned from Bob Wills? Everything!"

Above right: Left to right; Bill Woods, Luke Wills, Herb Henson, Johnny Cuviello, Bob Wills, and Oscar Whittington.

Above left: Columbia released Spade Cooley's ten-inch album *Sagebrush Swing* in 1949.

Above: Spade Cooley spent the 1940s packing Southern California ballrooms, including the Redondo Barn, which issued this show poster.

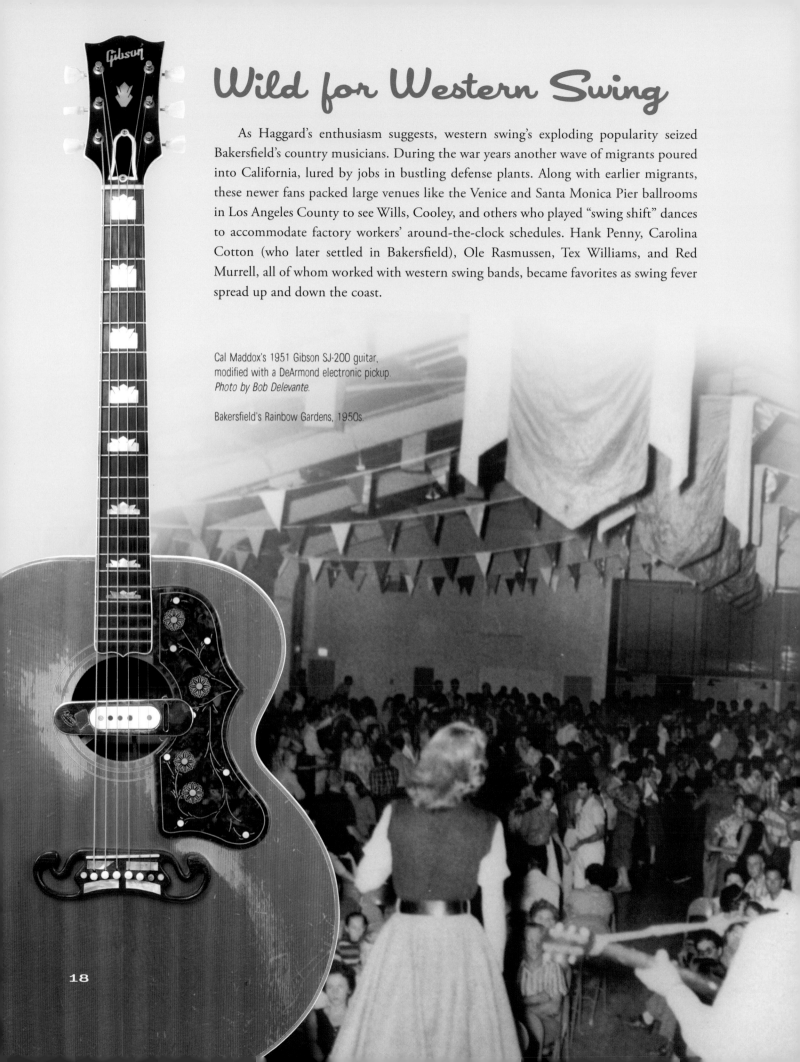

Wild for Western Swing

As Haggard's enthusiasm suggests, western swing's exploding popularity seized Bakersfield's country musicians. During the war years another wave of migrants poured into California, lured by jobs in bustling defense plants. Along with earlier migrants, these newer fans packed large venues like the Venice and Santa Monica Pier ballrooms in Los Angeles County to see Wills, Cooley, and others who played "swing shift" dances to accommodate factory workers' around-the-clock schedules. Hank Penny, Carolina Cotton (who later settled in Bakersfield), Ole Rasmussen, Tex Williams, and Red Murrell, all of whom worked with western swing bands, became favorites as swing fever spread up and down the coast.

Cal Maddox's 1951 Gibson SJ-200 guitar, modified with a DeArmond electronic pickup. *Photo by Bob Delevante.*

Bakersfield's Rainbow Gardens, 1950s.

FAMILY ROAMS U.S. FOR WORK

A hitch-hiking family of seven found shelter at Oakland's "Pipe City" after a cross-country trip from Alabama seeking work. The family comprises (left to right): **Calvin Maddux,** his father, **Charles; Rose, Fred** (standing), **Mrs. Lulu Maddux, Henry** and **Kenneth.** They have "ridden the rails" in their westward trek, and hope to make their home in California—*Tribune Photo.*
(reprinted from the Oakland Tribune, April 11, 1933)

Top: Cal, Henry, Rose, Don, and Fred Maddox, 1948.

Above: The Maddox family was featured in the *Oakland Tribune,* April 11, 1933.

Rose Maddox's satin western shirt, made by Nathan Turk.
Courtesy of Marty Stuart. Photo by Bob Delevante.

Bakersfield's Homegrown Scene

Entertainers such as T. Texas Tyler and Jimmy Wakely routinely traveled from Los Angeles to headline Bakersfield's big weekend dances, but by the late 1940s the local country community began to embrace its own stars. In January 1949 fiddler Jimmy Thomason, who had long played with Louisiana Governor Jimmie Davis's band, took over the Beardsley Ballroom's Saturday night dance and became one of the first professional musicians to set up shop in Bakersfield. Thomason released a handful of sides for King Records in the early '50s and hosted several incarnations of his locally televised *Jimmy Thomason Show.*

Sadly, the Beardsley Ballroom burned to the ground in 1950. "When Beardsley burned we girls just cried and cried," said Bakersfield native Joyce Simpson. "When it was gone we all went over to Rainbow Gardens." This venue was already staging Wednesday night dances featuring "Western Swing music with a boogie beat." The dance hall soon emerged as Bakersfield's new hotspot. About twelve miles out of town, Cousin Ebb Pilling ran the Pumpkin Center Barn Dance. A jeweler by day, Pilling dressed as a country rube and played banjo with his own group, in addition to hosting touring performers such as Modesto's Maddox Brothers and Rose.

Dubbed "The Most Colorful Hillbilly Band in America" for their flashy stage wear, the Maddoxes were an Alabama sharecropping family who moved to California in 1933 and became an important bridge between 1940s western swing and the growing honky-tonk movement that shaped the Bakersfield Sound in the 1950s. Fred Maddox later explained his band's use of amplification and electric instruments: "When you do that . . . [it] makes it rockabilly. At least that's what they called it. To me it's just good old country music." Merle Haggard recalled that the Maddoxes "had a little guitar player named Roy Nichols who was a couple years older than me, and I idolized him."

(continued on page 22)

BILL WOODS

He never toured as a headlining artist, released an album, or appeared on *Billboard*'s country charts, but Bill Woods is widely revered as the godfather of the Bakersfield Sound. "He furthered the careers of practically every artist that emanated from Bakersfield," Capitol Records producer Ken Nelson said of the tireless Woods, who filled the roles of bandleader, sideman, studio musician, disc jockey, manager, producer, and promoter. Hit-making Capitol artist Ferlin Husky agreed: "He was always running around trying to help everybody."

A multi-instrumentalist, Woods was raised in Texas migrant labor camps, where he soaked up various musical influences. "A Mexican family lived next door," he remembered, "and they played trumpets and guitars most every night out in front of their tent." By age fifteen, he joined a group called the Texas Hillbillies; in 1940, Woods moved with his family to California's San Joaquin Valley. He relocated to the San Francisco Bay area during World War II and formed the Texas Stars, a band including future Bakersfield television host Herb Henson.

Woods re-joined his family in Bakersfield in 1946, playing part time in Odell Johnson's band at the Rhythm Rancho. He launched the city's first DJ-hosted country show on radio station KAFY the following year, and soon formed the Orange Blossom Playboys. The group became the first Bakersfield country act to record commercially when they cut two sides for the Los Angeles–based Modern label in 1949. In 1950, Woods took over the house band at the Blackboard and became a staple at the storied Bakersfield nightspot. "I was there fourteen years, eight shifts a week," he recalled.

Above: Bill Woods in the 1950s. *Courtesy of Billy Mize and family.*

Left: Bill Woods's gold ring, with diamonds set into his initials. *Courtesy of Ray Urquhart. Photo by Bob Delevante.*

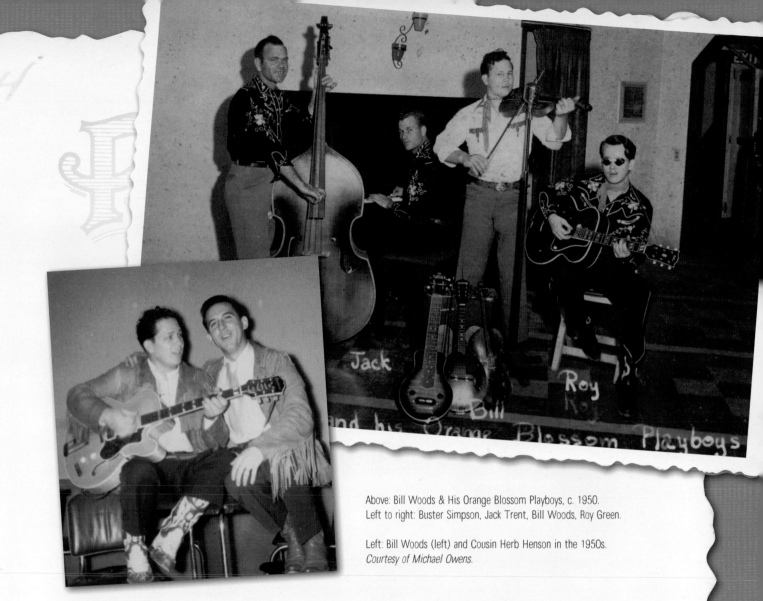

Above: Bill Woods & His Orange Blossom Playboys, c. 1950.
Left to right: Buster Simpson, Jack Trent, Bill Woods, Roy Green.

Left: Bill Woods (left) and Cousin Herb Henson in the 1950s.
Courtesy of Michael Owens.

It was Woods who convinced Herb Henson and Ferlin Husky to move to Bakersfield. During his Blackboard tenure, musicians Woods recruited for the band included Billy Mize, Merle Haggard, and Buck Owens, who served as vocalist and lead guitarist from 1951 until 1958. "He was really a wonderful recognizer of talent," Haggard stressed.

When he wasn't on the bandstand, Woods was putting up concert posters, calling DJs, booking talent, or playing on one of the five hundred recording sessions he estimated he'd worked. He held down a series of radio gigs, helped launch Henson's *Trading Post* TV series, hosted his own television show on KBAK, owned a variety of record labels, and produced dozens of local artists. "I didn't know what it was to have less than three jobs," Woods laughed.

In the mid-1960s a demolition derby accident sidelined him, but Woods eventually returned to music and toured with Merle Haggard, who recorded Red Simpson's tribute "Bill Woods from Bakersfield." In 1972, Woods recorded his signature number, Terry Fell's "Truck Drivin' Man," for Capitol. It would be the only major-label release for the man *Cowboy Songs* magazine described in 1956 as "one of those rare and charming fellows who would rather talk about other stars than about himself."

—*Scott B. Bomar*

Rehearsing at Bill Woods's home, c. 1953. Left to right (back row): Jean Shepard, Bill Woods, Johnny Cuviello, Fuzzy Owen; (front row): Gene Breeden, Lewis Talley, Jelly Sanders.

(from page 19)

From Big Bands to Small Clubs

While the Barn, the Pumpkin Center Barn Dance, the Beardsley Ballroom, and Rainbow Gardens kept dancers moving, a less formal brand of entertainment was taking hold during this same era. Musicians who admired Bob Wills's big band sound and Roy Nichols's hot guitar playing began combining both influences. Odell Johnson & His Rhythm Ranch Pals kicked off the grand opening of the Rhythm Rancho on Highway 99 in March 1946, signaling a transition from large dance halls to clubs where western swing would be re-imagined by small electrified combos. Bill Woods—who would later become the godfather of the city's music scene—moved to Bakersfield that same year and started sitting in with the house band after striking up a friendship with its fiddler, Oscar Whittington.

A talented multi-instrumentalist, Woods was also a tireless promoter and talent scout. By 1949, players were feeling his influence as they began to establish themselves at a handful of honky-tonks— including the Clover Club, the Lucky Spot, and the Sad Sack—that cropped up along Edison Highway on the outskirts of town. Two of the more influential musicians were Arkansas-born cousins Fuzzy Owen and Lewis Talley, who arrived in the late 1940s and worked the Sad Sack and Chester Avenue's Blackboard Cafe, where they backed Tex Butler.

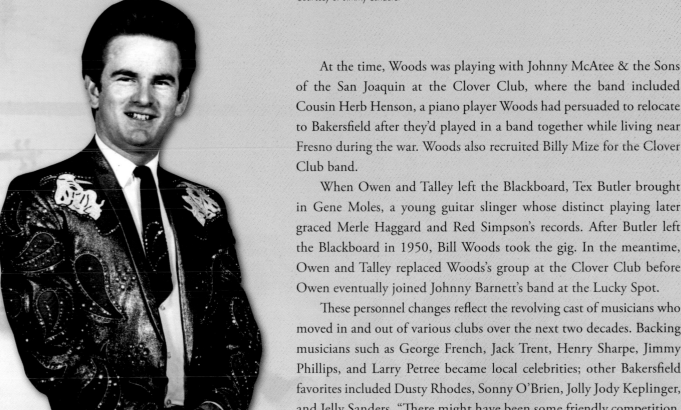

Above: Bill Woods's 1941 Martin O-18.
Courtesy of Ray Urquhart.
Photo by Bob Delevante.

Below: Bakersfield singer Bobby Durham,
who recorded for Capitol in the 1960s.

Jelly Sanders' Rhythm Rangers at the Sport Center in Porterville, California, 1948.
Left to right: Johnny Maynard, Jelly Sanders, Bob Autry, Frank (last name unknown),
unidentified accordion player, Connie Minnick, Buddy Jayroll.
Courtesy of Jimmy Sanders.

At the time, Woods was playing with Johnny McAtee & the Sons of the San Joaquin at the Clover Club, where the band included Cousin Herb Henson, a piano player Woods had persuaded to relocate to Bakersfield after they'd played in a band together while living near Fresno during the war. Woods also recruited Billy Mize for the Clover Club band.

When Owen and Talley left the Blackboard, Tex Butler brought in Gene Moles, a young guitar slinger whose distinct playing later graced Merle Haggard and Red Simpson's records. After Butler left the Blackboard in 1950, Bill Woods took the gig. In the meantime, Owen and Talley replaced Woods's group at the Clover Club before Owen eventually joined Johnny Barnett's band at the Lucky Spot.

These personnel changes reflect the revolving cast of musicians who moved in and out of various clubs over the next two decades. Backing musicians such as George French, Jack Trent, Henry Sharpe, Jimmy Phillips, and Larry Petree became local celebrities; other Bakersfield favorites included Dusty Rhodes, Sonny O'Brien, Jolly Jody Keplinger, and Jelly Sanders. "There might have been some friendly competition, but there was no rivalry," Fuzzy Owen explained. "We were all like family." Bobby Durham, who recorded for Capitol in the 1960s, agreed: "If somebody had a session we'd go down to L.A. and work on it. If somebody was sick, we'd all pull together."

23

Above: Bakersfield Sound pioneer Ralph Mooney, early 1960s.

Left: Buck Owens used this modified Fender Telecaster, with an early 1950s neck and a 1962 body, at recording sessions and performances.
Courtesy of Buck Owens' Crystal Palace. Photo by Bob Delevante.

Western Swing Meets Hillbilly with an Electric Guitar

According to fiddler Oscar Whittington, the Bakersfield Sound began to gel in the late 1940s and early 1950s. "The Bakersfield Sound is western swing meets hillbilly with an electric guitar," he explained in 2007. "We were all into western swing, but along came Fuzzy Owen and Lewis Talley, and they were just hillbillies from Arkansas. We were all trying to play together and had to learn how to make it work."

With the invention of better sound systems and solid-body electric guitars—primarily Fender's iconic Telecaster—small groups of four or five musicians could easily cut through the din of rowdy honky-tonks and keep crowds dancing all night. "We didn't know we were making a Bakersfield Sound," laughed guitarist Tommy Hays, who arrived in town in February 1947. "We were just playing music. . . . [It had] more of a bite to it. . . . [T]he Fender guitar . . . had a tremendous effect on the sound because it's a sharp sound, a treble sound." Musicians joked that the Telecaster's solid-body construction both minimized feedback at high volumes and allowed the sturdy instrument to double as a weapon in rough-and-tumble clubs. The importance of the electric guitar to Bakersfield's music cannot be overstated. Buck Owens and his lead guitarist Don Rich—along with Roy Nichols, Gene Moles, Gene Breeden, and others—bent and twisted their notes to great effect, just as Bakersfield guitar makers like Mosrite's Semie Moseley crafted sought-after instruments.

Additionally, the piercing tones and aggressive playing of local pedal steel guitarists Fuzzy Owen, Billy Mize, the Buckaroos' Tom Brumley, and Leo LeBlanc shaped Bakersfield's music. In crafting the Bakersfield Sound, however, the most influential steel guitarist was Ralph Mooney, who won recognition for his work with Wynn Stewart, Buck Owens, and Merle Haggard.

Joe Maphis's trademark double-neck electric guitar, custom made by Semie Moseley in 1954.
Photo by Bob Delevante.

Bakersfield's most famous honky-tonk, the Blackboard Cafe.

The Blackboard's Big Beat

As honky-tonks eclipsed large dance halls, the Blackboard became the city's foremost nightspot. It was the loudest, liveliest, smokiest, and, some say, most dangerous club around when Bill Woods's band—with Buck Owens on guitar and vocals—held court there for the better part of the 1950s. Blaring guitar amps, frequent fistfights, and the occasional shooting or stabbing solidified the Blackboard's reputation as the ultimate rough-hewn honky-tonk. "You could count on three or four fights every night," Woods confirmed, "and there were a couple of killings while I was there."

When Woods took over the band from Tex Butler in 1950, the club was still a small bar and café, but his growing popularity led to expansion. "While we was there they added on to the Blackboard twice," Woods said, "and it would hold probably . . . six hundred or a little more people." Don Markham, who joined Woods's band in 1955 and went on to play with Merle Haggard, experienced Woods's appeal firsthand: "He was a marvelous guy. You felt like you knew him after five minutes. He spent half his time talking with the people, leaning over the edge of the bandstand."

"We were not used to people dancing when you were performing," remembered Rose Lee Maphis, who moved to the Golden State with her husband and musical partner, Joe, in 1951. The first date Joe played after relocating to California was at the Blackboard. "It was the loudest band I have ever heard in my life," he recalled. "I had never worked with drums or electrical instruments. The smoke was thick, and I wasn't used to that." Struck by the new experience, Maphis wrote a song while driving home to Los Angeles that night. "Dim Lights, Thick Smoke (and Loud, Loud Music)" not only became a honky-tonk staple, but also perfectly described what made the Blackboard different from Richmond's *Old Dominion Barn Dance* (where the Maphises had been regulars) or Nashville's Grand Ole Opry. "[We] played on the edge of speed, edge of making the beat go faster," Buck Owens later emphasized, "where it made you want to shut up and dance, baby."

Cocktail waitress vest from the Blackboard Cafe.
Courtesy of Buck Owens' Crystal Palace. Photo by Bob Delevante.

Putting It All Together

An early incarnation of Bill Woods's Orange Blossom Playboys had been the first Bakersfield country group to record commercially when they released "Trusting You" and "Have I Got a Chance with You" on the Los Angeles–based Modern label in 1949. Billy Mize played steel guitar while Cliff Crofford (who would later pen hits such as Walter Brennan's "Old Rivers" and Merle Haggard and Clint Eastwood's "Bar Room Buddies") handled vocal and trumpet duties. The recording captures the small combo version of western swing that dominated area clubs early in the city's heyday. As rockabilly and rock & roll emerged, these influences also affected Bakersfield musicians.

Woods patterned his guitar playing after that of Bob Wills sideman Junior Barnard. "[Barnard] had an aggressive, hard-swinging style that was like rock & roll for its time," Wills veteran Jimmy Wyble told *Guitar Player* in 1983. Indeed, rock & roll was an important element of the Blackboard's success. "Buck and I would go down to this record store that was kind of a black record store on California Avenue," Don Markham recalled. "So, really, the main influence in the Bakersfield Sound was bringing black music and rock & roll and rockabilly into the country music we were playing at the club." Owens himself described the Bakersfield Sound as "a mix of Bob Wills and the Texas Playboys and Little Richard."

(continued on page 30)

Left: Bill Woods's pioneering 1949 release on Modern Records.

Right to left: Blackboard bandleader Bill Woods stands outside the nightclub with Herb Henson, Billy Mize, and an unidentified friend, early 1950s.

PLAY IT LOUD

It was not just coincidence or a matter of taste that the electric guitar played a dominant role in defining the Bakersfield Sound. As the popularity of large western-swing bands faded after World War II, smaller groups became the norm in California's dance halls, nightclubs, and honky-tonks. To cut through the crowd noise, guitarists required volume and a more powerful sound.

California emerged as a hotbed of electric guitar makers and innovators who designed and built instruments more suitable for live performance. The solid-body electric and steel guitars they made gave Bakersfield's country musicians the edge they needed and a sound they liked.

Paul Bigsby, of Downey, California, was one such innovator. Combining a background in industrial manufacturing with his love of music, he collaborated with recording star and guitar virtuoso Merle Travis to build a solid-body electric guitar that matched the sustain of a steel guitar.

The cover of this 1954 LP by Speedy West and Jimmy Bryant depicts these innovative West Coast session musicians and performers with the Fender Broadcaster guitar and custom-built Bigsby pedal steel the duo used on many of their exhilarating instrumental duets.

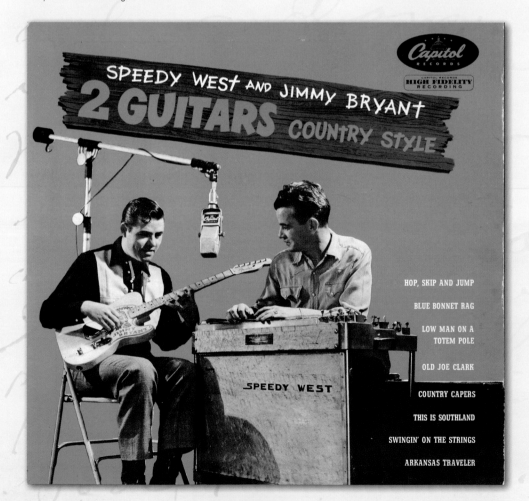

Above: California electronics engineer Bob Crook designed and built Standel custom amplifiers, prized by Chet Atkins, Hank Garland, Speedy West, and other top session guitarists. This Standel 25L15 model with green upholstery was made in 1953 for Joe Maphis, a staff guitarist on Los Angeles TV program *Town Hall Party. Courtesy of Jody Maphis. Photo by Bob Delevante.*

Above right: Based on a design by Merle Travis and built by Paul Bigsby in 1947, this was one of the first solid-body electric guitars made.

Bigsby's custom-made guitars were revolutionary, but it took the shrewd business know-how of Fullerton's Leo Fender to get a similar, more affordable design into the hands of working musicians. His guitars matched the improvements of Bigsby and Travis's design, but were also basic enough in construction to mass produce.

In 1949, Fender developed the prototype of his Telecaster model. The Telecaster's simplicity of design and distinct, treble tone have made it one of the most popular guitars of all time. It was the guitar of choice for Merle Haggard, Roy Nichols, Buck Owens, Don Rich, and other Bakersfield pickers.

—*Museum Staff*

(from page 27)

A Town South of Bakersfield

The powerful musical blend heard in the Blackboard and other Bakersfield nightspots might have remained an isolated regional phenomenon if not for the established entertainment industry in nearby Los Angeles. Building on foundations laid by the Beverly Hill Billies, Stuart Hamblen, Patsy Montana, and other radio and recording artists of the late 1920s and early 1930s, Gene Autry and his fellow big-screen singing cowboys helped define Hollywood as a country music capital well before Nashville's rise to prominence in the late 1940s. Their smooth western songs and custom-embroidered, rhinestone-accented stage wear, designed by tailors such as Nathan Turk and Nudie Cohn, helped forge the flashy West Coast cowboy archetype that served as a counterpoint to the rural hillbilly image common in early country music.

By 1949, Pasadena's KXLA became one of the first all-country format radio stations in America. During the 1950s, Los Angeles TV shows like *Town Hall Party* and Cliffie Stone's *Hometown Jamboree* enjoyed large audiences and made household names of California-based artists like Tennessee Ernie Ford and Merle Travis. Stone was closely associated with Capitol Records as a talent scout and producer, and was a partner in Central Songs, a music publishing firm he co-owned with Capitol A&R men Ken Nelson and Lee Gillette. Stone and Nelson were power brokers in a growing West Coast country industry that boosted rising stars including Skeets McDonald and Wynn Stewart. Innovative musicians such as Jimmy Bryant, one of the first to adopt the Fender Telecaster guitar, and Speedy West, whose untamed pedal steel guitar style captured the edgy excitement of West Coast country, worked hundreds of sessions for Capitol and played in the house band on *Hometown Jamboree*.

Bakersfield's Capitol Connection

Another *Hometown Jamboree* favorite was Ferlin Husky, who had first recorded as Terry Preston for Pasadena's Four Star label in the late 1940s. "When I was in Los Angeles," Husky recounted, "Bill Woods came down for something, and he was telling me about Bakersfield." Husky moved north in 1951, landing a daily radio program on Bakersfield's KBIS and appearing weekly at Rainbow Gardens. "Ferlin was the first major artist . . . in Bakersfield to have any kind of name," Tommy Collins stressed. Husky became the first Bakersfield singer to record for Capitol and, on May 19, 1953, he was the bandleader and duet partner on Jean Shepard's second Capitol recording session. He brought in Fuzzy Owen, Lewis Talley, Bill Woods, and Tommy Collins to accompany her on "A Dear John Letter," which featured Husky's recitations. That year, "Dear John" became a #1 country smash and climbed to #4 on *Billboard*'s pop chart.

During the 1950s and '60s Bakersfield developed into a rich resource for Ken Nelson, who relied on Bakersfield pickers to back Wynn Stewart, the Collins Kids, and other singers. "In fact almost any day will see some of [the city's musicians] driving over the Ridge Route, 99, headed for a session in Hollywood," *Country and Western Jamboree* reported in 1955. According to Fuzzy Owen, it was Nelson who first coined the term "Bakersfield Sound" to describe their aggressive style of playing. As Buck Owens emphasized in 1989, "Maybe it's not hardly as smooth, or as sweet or as slick, but it sure enough is human."

Other Bakersfield talent joined the Capitol fold as the fifties progressed. The label issued seven Herb Henson singles, beginning in 1952. The following year, Ferlin Husky played lead guitar on Tommy Collins's first Capitol session, but was replaced by Buck Owens after Husky's own career took off. Collins notched six Top Twenty country singles in 1954 and 1955, and Owens's biting Telecaster leads on "Whatcha Gonna Do Now," "It Tickles," and other Collins sides exposed a national audience to the Bakersfield Sound. A teenaged Dallas Frazier released several Capitol singles in 1954.

The Farmer Boys, featuring Farmersville, California's Bobby Adamson and Woody Murray, were discovered by Herb Henson and performed regularly on his popular *Trading Post* Bakersfield TV show. Starting in 1955, the duo recorded four sessions for Capitol with backing groups including, at various points, Tally, Owen, Woods, Jelly Sanders, Roy Nichols, and Johnny Cuviello, a drummer who had worked with Bob Wills's Texas Playboys before joining the house band at the Blackboard. At the Farmer Boys' final session, in February of 1957, Norm Hamlet and Gene Breeden made their debuts as major-label studio sidemen. After the recording date, Ken Nelson signed the session's rhythm guitar player, Buck Owens, as a featured Capitol artist.

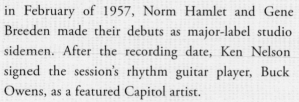

Below: Ken Nelson and Buck Owens chat during a session at Capitol Records Tower.

Right: Capitol's iconic building opened in 1956 at the corner of Hollywood Boulevard and Vine Street. *Photos courtesy of Capitol/EMI.*

Bakersfield's Music Business Boom

As the buzz began to grow about the Bakersfield music community, new independent labels appeared. Bill Woods and Johnny Cuviello teamed with local businessman Chris Christensen to launch Bakersfield Records and the associated Fire imprint. Among other artists, the partners recorded Phil Baugh, Coy Baker, Louise Duncan, Tommy Duncan, Lawton Jiles, and Gene Martin & the Desert Stars—Gene Breeden and Norm Hamlet's group. Throughout the 1950s and '60s labels such as Audan, Global, Hillcrest, Rose, Rural Rhythm, Santa Fe, Starview, Stereotone, and Wilco issued discs by local favorites including Tom Brumley's brother, Al Brumley Jr.; Anita Cross; Kenny Hayes; Billy Mize's brother, Buddy—later a successful Nashville songwriter—and Gene Moles.

Other important Bakersfield recording companies included Pike, Mosrite, and multiple labels associated with flamboyant producer Gary S. Paxton. Owned by Leon Hart and Roy Flowers, Pike released singles by Flowers's wife, Vancie, an artist formerly signed to the Los Angeles–based Crest label. Flowers's Crest labelmate Tommy Dee, who cut the #11 pop hit "Three Stars" in 1959, moved to Bakersfield in the 1960s and recorded for Pike before organizing his own Three Stars label. In addition, Pike was the debut label for a pre-teen Ronnie Sessions, who eventually moved to Nashville and recorded fifteen charting country singles for the MGM and MCA labels.

Bakersfield Records was one of several independent labels in the city in the 1960s. Gene Martin was actually Bakersfield musician Gene Breeden.

Barbara Mandrell's first record, "Queen for a Day," was released in 1966 on Mosrite Records, an independent label owned by the Moseley brothers in Bakersfield.

Rose Lee Maphis's 1939 Martin D-18 was heavily modified by Semie Moseley, who added a custom pickguard, bridge, volume and tone controls, Bigsby neck, and Mosrite peghead. *Courtesy of Rose Lee Maphis. Photo by Bob Delevante.*

While in Bakersfield, Sessions also recorded for Mosrite Records, established by brothers Semie and Andy Moseley following the initial success of their guitar manufacturing business. In addition to sides by Barbara Mandrell, Mosrite released discs by Eddie Dean, Tommy Duncan, Doyle Holly (of Owens's Buckaroos), Joe and Rose Lee Maphis, and Gene Moles. Among the first to adopt the Mosrite guitar, the Maphises moved to Bakersfield from Los Angeles in the early 1960s to join the cast of *Cousin Herb's Trading Post.*

Gary S. Paxton established his reputation as an L.A. pop producer with Dallas Frazier's "Alley Oop," a 1960 hit for the Hollywood Argyles, and Bobby "Boris" Pickett's 1962 chart topper "The Monster Mash." Relocating to Bakersfield in 1967, Paxton opened the first modern recording facility in Kern County. His loyal group of studio stalwarts included keyboardist Rick Davis (whose son Jonathan would found the highly successful Bakersfield-based rock group Korn in the 1990s), multi-instrumentalist Dennis Payne, bassist and guitarist Kenny Johnson, and future Byrds guitarist Clarence White. Paxton's studio team helped generate numerous sides for his various small labels. Among them was the Gosdin Brothers' Top Forty country single "Hangin' On" (co-written by Buddy Mize), which appeared on Paxton's Bakersfield International Records (which, despite the name, was based in Los Angeles). Released in 1967, "Hangin' On" was the first charting disc for future country hitmaker Vern Gosdin.

Ronnie Sessions in the late 1960s. Sessions, who began performing on *Cousin Herb's Trading Post* at age nine, later attained country chart success with "Ambush" and other 1970s hits.

Harlan Howard (above) used this Underwood SX-100 typewriter,
made c. 1952, to type lyrics to his songs.
Courtesy of Melanie Smith Howard. Photo by Bob Delevante.

Below: Fuzzy Owen's Fender 1000 double-neck pedal steel guitar.
Courtesy of Fuzzy Owen. Photo by Bob Delevante.

FUZZY OWEN

Lewis Talley & the Oklahoma Roundup, c. 1949. Left to right: Bill Burhler, George French, Lewis Talley, Tex Butler, Fuzzy Owen.

A Tally of Hits

By far, Bakersfield's most successful homegrown label was Tally Records. Thanks in part to their earnings as credited writers of "A Dear John Letter," Lewis Talley and Fuzzy Owen started their company in 1956 and released a handful of singles by artists including Cliff Crofford, Herb Henson, Red Simpson, Wally Lewis, Al Hendrix, and Lucky Spot bandleader Johnny Barnett. Tally also recorded Harlan Howard, an up-and-coming Los Angeles songwriter who co-wrote hits with Buck Owens before moving east and earning a reputation as "the Dean of Nashville Songwriters." Bobby Austin's original recording of "Apartment #9" was an especially important Tally release. Penned by Austin and Johnny Paycheck, the song later became Tammy Wynette's first single for Epic Records, in 1966.

In 1963, Tally made its most significant contribution to country music by signing Merle Haggard. "Lewis Talley and Fuzzy Owen were my two closest friends in the business," Haggard reflected. "Lewis really babied me and looked out for me and taught me how to dress, how to carry myself, and those kinds of things. He was like a big brother to me."

Thanks to releases by Austin, Haggard, and Bonnie Owens, Tally was the only label headquartered in Bakersfield to appear on *Billboard*'s country singles chart. When Haggard took Liz Anderson's "(My Friends Are Gonna Be) Strangers" to #10 in 1965, Ken Nelson signed him to Capitol, where he scored twenty-four #1 hits. Haggard racked up an additional fourteen #1s for MCA and Epic in the late 1970s and 1980s.

(continued on page 38)

TOMMY COLLINS

In 1952, Leonard Sipes visited Bakersfield with his girlfriend, future rockabilly star Wanda Jackson, and her parents. Both Sipes and Jackson were known in Oklahoma City for their appearances on radio station KLPR, and Sipes had already released two singles on Morgan Records. Impressed by Bakersfield's music scene, however, he decided to stay.

When Leonard Sipes met Ferlin Husky, who was performing as Terry Preston at the Rainbow Gardens, Husky hired him on the spot, later gave him the stage name Tommy Collins, and helped him get work playing guitar on Hollywood sessions for Capitol Records. "He flat gave me an introduction to the entertainment business," Collins later affirmed.

By 1953, Collins had signed an artist's contract with Capitol. He selected Buck Owens to play lead guitar on most of his early recordings. "I think that choice puts him well into the crowd of people who are responsible for that Bakersfield sound," Merle Haggard stated in 1992. "Buck put that little lead guitar riff in . . . and it became a trademark of mine," Collins explained. After his self-penned "You Better Not Do That" reached #2 in 1954, Collins made a guest appearance on the Grand Ole Opry. For Owens, backing his friend on that date remained a career highlight.

Left: Tommy Collins and Buck Owens at Capitol's Hollywood studio, c. 1954. *Courtesy of Buck Owens Private Foundation and Capitol/EMI.*

Below: Typed lyrics, with handwritten corrections, to Tommy Collins's song "Today, All My Sad Songs Came True," published by Merle Haggard's Shade Tree Music. *Courtesy of Michael Owens.*

```
                    TODAY, ALL MY SAD SONGS CAME TRUE

                                                    Tommy Collins
                                                    Shade Tree Music
    A
    SINCE MY YOUTH I'VE TAKEN WORDS AND MADE THEM RHYME
    A
    JUST A HOBBY THAT I CHOSE TO PASS THE TIME
    HAPPY SONGS AND SAD SONGS ABOUT WHERE LOVE WENT WRONG
    BUT THEY WERE ALWAYS JUST SOME MADE UP THOUGHTS OF MINE
    LIKE THIS GUY HIGH ON A HILLTOP, LOOKIN' DOWN
    WHERE HIS GIRL IS WITH SOMEONE SOMEWHERE IN TOWN
    I NEVER THOUGHT THAT SONGS LIKE THIS COULD APPLY TO ME AND YOU
    BUT, TODAY, ALL MY SAD SONGS CAME TRUE

    BRIDGE:
    TODAY, ALL MY SAD SONGS CAME TRUE
    I'M LIVING THOSE LINES THAT HAD NO MEANING TILL I LOST YOU
    I'VE OFTEN SAID, WAKE UP DARLING,   HERES A SONG I
    YOU MUST HAVE UNDERSTOOD EACH WORD AND EVERY NOTE   WROTE
    I'VE HEARD YOU SAY "YOU TOLD IT RIGHT"
                                      BUT REALLY I NEVER KNEW
    UNTIL  TODAY WHEN ALL MY SAD SONGS CAME TRUE
```

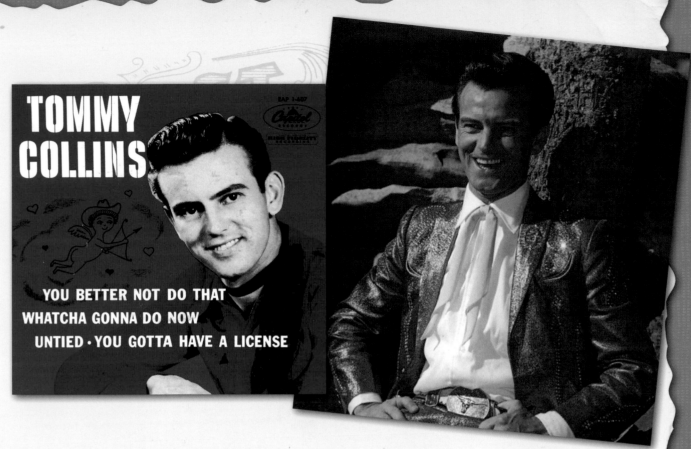

Left: Tommy Collins's first four Top Ten hits were re-packaged on this 45-rpm extended-play record in 1955.

Right: Tommy Collins in the 1960s.

Three more Collins originals became Top Ten records in 1954–55. Then, in 1957, Collins began preparing for the ministry. Preaching became his primary focus, and by 1960 he'd lost his record deal. Three years later he began spending time with Merle Haggard. "Tommy Collins was a great influence on me as a songwriter," Haggard reflected. Thanks to their friendship, Collins re-signed with Capitol in 1963.

Buck Owens released an entire album of Tommy Collins songs that year, but it seemed that Collins's moment had passed. Unable to land any hits, he signed with Columbia in 1965 and started recording in Nashville. "It was very difficult to keep the Buck Owens sound going," Collins acknowledged. He gained one hit ("If You Can't Bite, Don't Growl") and toured with Owens's road show, but alcoholism and depression soon set in.

By the early 1980s, Collins was sober, and in 1981 Merle Haggard reached *Billboard's* Top Ten with "Leonard," a tribute to his old friend. In 1999, Collins was inducted into the Nashville Songwriters Hall of Fame in recognition of hits he'd written, including his own "Whatcha Gonna Do Now" (1954), Haggard's "The Roots of My Raising" (1976) and "Carolyn" (1971), and "If You Ain't Lovin' (You Ain't Livin')" (Faron Young, 1955; George Strait, 1988).

—*Scott B. Bomar*

(from page 35)

Big on the Small Screen

Nelson first met Haggard in September 1963 when the producer journeyed to Bakersfield's Civic Auditorium to record a concert celebrating ten years of Cousin Herb Henson's *Trading Post*. In addition to Johnny Bond, Glen Campbell, Roy Clark, Tommy Collins, Rose Maddox, Buck Owens, Jean Shepard, and Merle Travis, the resulting album, *Country Music Hootenanny*, showcased Buddy Cagle, the Kentucky Colonels, Joe and Rose Lee Maphis, Bob Morris, and Roy Nichols. Such an aggregation of high-profile talent underscored television's importance in Bakersfield's country community.

The city's first country television program was KAFY-TV's *The Jimmy and Louise Thomason Show*, whose initial broadcast, in 1953, featured Tommy Collins, Cliff Crofford, Wanda Jackson, Gene Moles, Fuzzy Owen, Bonnie Owens, and Jean Shepard. Soon after the Thomasons' program debuted, Henson began hosting his *Trading Post* series on KERO-TV. In 1955, Billy Mize and Cliff Crofford began *Chuck Wagon Gang*, which gave Merle Haggard his first television exposure. "Buck was the lead guitarist on there and Billy invited me on the show," Haggard elaborated. "That was the first time I ever met Buck Owens. I was just a teenager and I sang 'King Without a Queen' that Lefty Frizzell had out at that time."

Bakersfield country TV programs continued throughout the 1960s. Among them were various configurations of Jimmy Thomason's show and programs hosted by Jelly Sanders, Tommy Dee, and Wes Sanders & His Hoedown Gang. Following Henson and Thomason, perhaps the best known Bakersfield country television MC was Dave Stogner, a western swing mainstay from Fresno who had recorded for the Decca label.

Dave Stogner and his Western Swing Band on the set of their Bakersfield TV program, 1960s.
Left to right: Red Simpson, Pat Rush, Daryl Stogner, Ray Salter, Norm Hamlet, Dave Stogner.

Buck Owens and the Buckaroos, c. 1966. Left to right: Tom Brumley, Don Rich, Buck Owens, Willie Cantu, Doyle Holly.
Photos courtesy of Capitol/EMI.

Bolero jacket, with embroidery and rhinestones, made for Buck Owens by Nathan Turk.
Courtesy of Buck Owens' Crystal Palace.
Photo by Bob Delevante.

Country Music Capital of the West

By the late 1960s Buck Owens and Merle Haggard were superstars, and Ferlin Husky, Jean Shepard, Tommy Collins, Bonnie Owens, Billy Mize, and Red Simpson had all achieved national recognition. The Blackboard, the Lucky Spot, Tex's Barrel House, and various local television shows provided abundant work for musicians, and fans had numerous options for live entertainment seven nights a week.

Meanwhile, Buck Owens had built a sizable music empire based in Bakersfield. Among other businesses, Buck Owens Enterprises comprised radio stations, a management firm, a modern recording studio, a music publishing company, and a booking agency.

Although Haggard, Dick Curless, Red Simpson, and other artists affiliated with Owens's companies in the '60s eventually moved on, Owens built a new stable of entertainers such as Buck and Bonnie's son Buddy Alan, the Hager Twins, Freddie Hart, Lawanda Lindsay, Susan Raye, and Sheb Wooley. Others included the Bakersfield Brass, Tony Booth, Homer Joy, Faye Hardin, Rodney Lay, Bob Morris, and Mayf Nutter.

Some journalists began referring to Bakersfield as "Nashville West" in recognition of its expanding country music industry. In 1967 *Billboard* featured a lengthy profile of Bakersfield titled "Country Music Capitol of the West." Four years later, an influential *Los Angeles Times* story further solidified the public's perception of Bakersfield as a growing country music center with the potential to rival Nashville. On April 26, 1972, the Country Music Association (CMA) attracted more than six hundred members for a three-day convention at the Bakersfield Inn, with Mayor Don Hart officially proclaiming "Country Music Week" in honor of the occasion. In 1973, journalist Richard Kleiner asserted that "Bakersfield is about ready to challenge Nashville, Tennessee, as the country music capital of the world." Jack McFadden, Owens's manager, predicted that "in ten years Chester Avenue will be Music Row West. This place is going to explode."

The Music and the Magic Fade

Within a few years, however, it all came crashing down. Bickering, competition, territorialism, and legal wrangling replaced the family atmosphere fostered by the city's country music pioneers. By the 1980s, Owens had stopped recording, even though he continued to co-host *Hee Haw* into 1986. Haggard had moved his home and his businesses out of town before the decade began. Country music could still be heard in Bakersfield, but there was a growing recognition that the magic was slipping away.

Local musicians have offered various theories for Bakersfield's failure to sustain itself as a country music hub in the 1970s and beyond. Some point to an increase in television ownership and programming choices, which gradually kept more people at home instead of dancing in area clubs. Others cite stricter drunk-driving laws, which may have kept some patrons from their favorite honky-tonks. Still others maintain that if major music publishers and record labels had set up offices there, Bakersfield's music industry would have survived.

Perhaps Bakersfield simply lost sight of what made it distinct. It was always a live music town, but many in the business hoped to challenge Nashville's model by duplicating it—focusing on music publishing and major-label recording contracts rather than cultivating the city's own proud legacy. While Bakersfield's music scene floundered, Austin rose to prominence as an updated version of what Bakersfield had been: a specialized music community rooted in live performance. "Now that the hype has subsided," wrote local columnist Bryce Martin in 1984, "people are realizing that there was and is no 'Nashville West.' Rather, there is a rich and ongoing Bakersfield musical heritage."

At his Grand Ole Opry induction in 2001, Brad Paisley paid tribute to his hero Buck Owens by appearing in the Nathan Turk jacket Owens wore at his 1966 Carnegie Hall concert. Left to right: Steve Wariner, Brad Paisley, Bill Rains.
Photography by Randy Piland. Courtesy of the Grand Ole Opry Archives.

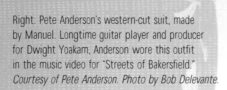

Right: Pete Anderson's western-cut suit, made by Manuel. Longtime guitar player and producer for Dwight Yoakam, Anderson wore this outfit in the music video for "Streets of Bakersfield." *Courtesy of Pete Anderson. Photo by Bob Delevante.*

Far Right: Dwight Yoakam wore this outfit on the cover of his 1988 album *Buenas Noches from a Lonely Room*, which included the #1 hit "Streets of Bakersfield." *Courtesy of Dwight Yoakam. Photo by Bob Delevante.*

An Enduring Legacy

In the 1980s, as Bakersfield's flame was flickering low, a wave of roots-minded performers like Ricky Skaggs, George Strait, and Randy Travis ushered in country's new-traditionalist movement by combining classic country sounds with a modern sensibility. Dwight Yoakam, the most outspoken champion of the Bakersfield Sound, achieved his first #1 hit when he coaxed Buck Owens out of retirement to join him on "Streets of Bakersfield" in 1988. Their duet symbolized the passing of the baton to a new generation who integrated key aspects of Bakersfield's music into their own styles.

Since then, artists such as Yoakam, Marty Stuart, the Mavericks, the Derailers, Dale Watson, Gary Allan, and Brad Paisley have continued to crank up their Telecasters and remind country fans what was great about Bakersfield's golden era. "If you had a little edge on you, if you had a little cowboy on you, if you were a bit of an innovator or a wildcat, you could stand a chance of making it more in California than in Nashville," Stuart explained. As long as there is country music, there will be a place for the twang of the Telecaster, the cry of the steel guitar, and the fiercely independent spirit that, for a brief time, made Bakersfield the Country Music Capital of the West. ∎

WYNN STEWART

Though he never lived in Bakersfield, Wynn Stewart strongly influenced the Bakersfield Sound. In 1955 Capitol recording artist Skeets McDonald brought the Los Angeles–based Stewart to the attention of producer Ken Nelson. "Ken contacted me by telephone," Stewart recalled, "auditioned me, and signed me to a contract on the spot, right there on the phone."

In early 1956, Stewart recorded his first Capitol session with assistance from Ralph Mooney, whose musicianship was central to Stewart's style. "It was Wynn who really invented my sound on steel guitar," Mooney explained. "I hit that rolling sound and he said, 'That's it!'" Stewart quickly gained a reputation among fellow artists as a "singer's singer" with a uniquely West Coast edge. According to Merle Haggard, "Wynn's sound was what influenced Buck and me both."

McDonald also put Stewart in touch with budding songwriter Harlan Howard. Stewart was the first artist to record a Howard song and was instrumental in launching Howard's first successful writing partnership. "Wynn drove me to Bakersfield," Howard recounted, "and introduced me to Buck Owens."

By 1959, Stewart had moved to Challenge Records, where he released several singles. In 1960, Owens notched a #3 country hit by covering Stewart's version of Howard's "Above and Beyond." Using Ralph Mooney on his early sessions, Owens found success with a sound similar to Stewart's.

From 1961 through 1964, Stewart appeared nightly at Las Vegas's Nashville Nevada Club; his

Left: Wynn Stewart and Jackie Burns at Stewart's Nashville Nevada Club in Las Vegas, 1960s.

Below: Wynn Stewart, 1969.
Courtesy of Linda Mooney Yates.

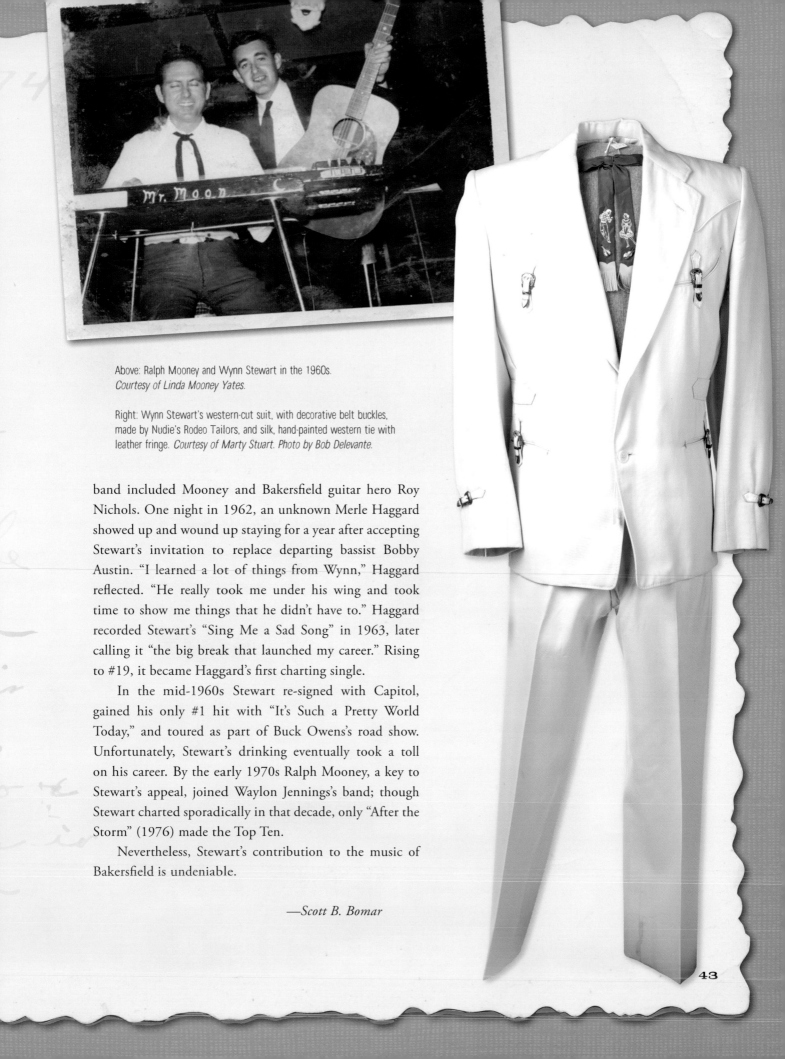

Above: Ralph Mooney and Wynn Stewart in the 1960s. *Courtesy of Linda Mooney Yates.*

Right: Wynn Stewart's western-cut suit, with decorative belt buckles, made by Nudie's Rodeo Tailors, and silk, hand-painted western tie with leather fringe. *Courtesy of Marty Stuart. Photo by Bob Delevante.*

band included Mooney and Bakersfield guitar hero Roy Nichols. One night in 1962, an unknown Merle Haggard showed up and wound up staying for a year after accepting Stewart's invitation to replace departing bassist Bobby Austin. "I learned a lot of things from Wynn," Haggard reflected. "He really took me under his wing and took time to show me things that he didn't have to." Haggard recorded Stewart's "Sing Me a Sad Song" in 1963, later calling it "the big break that launched my career." Rising to #19, it became Haggard's first charting single.

In the mid-1960s Stewart re-signed with Capitol, gained his only #1 hit with "It's Such a Pretty World Today," and toured as part of Buck Owens's road show. Unfortunately, Stewart's drinking eventually took a toll on his career. By the early 1970s Ralph Mooney, a key to Stewart's appeal, joined Waylon Jennings's band; though Stewart charted sporadically in that decade, only "After the Storm" (1976) made the Top Ten.

Nevertheless, Stewart's contribution to the music of Bakersfield is undeniable.

—*Scott B. Bomar*

FROM THE BACK ROADS OF TEXAS TO THE STREETS OF BAKERSFIELD

Left: Buck Owens, early 1950s.
Courtesy of Buddy Alan Owens.

Right: Buck Owens, c. 1965.

Below: Young Buck, c. 1939.
Courtesy of Buck Owens Private Foundation.

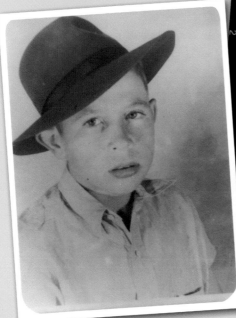

The Musical Journey of Buck Owens

By Randy Poe

He was born in Texas and grew up in Arizona, but for Buck Owens, Bakersfield, California, was home. Unlike the vast majority of country singers, songwriters, and musicians who have worked and lived in Nashville, the often rebellious and always independent Owens chose to create his own brand of country music some 2,000 miles away from Music City—racking up a remarkable twenty-one #1 hits along the way. In the process he helped give birth to a new country sound and did more than any other individual to establish Bakersfield as a country music center.

Beginnings

The second child of sharecroppers Alvis Edgar and Maicie Azel Owens, Alvis Edgar "Buck" Owens Jr. was born in Sherman, Texas, on August 12, 1929, just two months before the Wall Street crash and the onset of the Great Depression. At age three, young Owens informed his parents that he wished to be known as Buck—the same name as the family mule. In November 1937, not unlike a scene from *The Grapes of Wrath*, Buck's family headed west in search of better prospects. By this time there were four Owens children—Mary, Buck, Melvin, and Dorothy. In addition to the immediate family, Buck's Uncle Vernon Ellington and Aunt Lucille; their son, Jimmy; and Maicie's mother, Mary Myrtle, all piled into a 1933 Ford sedan with a trailer hooked on the back.

The group originally planned to resettle in California, but it was not to be. They had only reached Phoenix when the trailer hitch broke. Having relatives in nearby Mesa, the family decided to make Arizona their temporary home. As things turned out, it would remain their residence for more than a decade.

Buck's parents gave him a mandolin when he was in his early teens and, later, a Regal acoustic guitar. By 1945, now proficient on both instruments, he landed his first job in radio. Along with his friend Theryl Ray Britten, Owens secured a fifteen-minute slot on Mesa's KTYL. The duo billed themselves as Buck & Britt. The show paid nothing, but it led to steady gigs around Mesa, giving Owens valuable experience performing in front of a live audience—and a way to make money without toiling at manual labor in the hot Arizona sun.

Owens had endured grinding poverty, and he was determined to better himself. To succeed as a working musician, he built upon the stringband and cowboy sounds he heard on radio, and he mastered western swing, rhythm & blues, and honky-tonk—anything to please the crowds he entertained at local clubs and dance halls.

Top: Buck Owens and his sister Mary, c. 1937
Courtesy of Buck Owens Private Foundation.

Above: Young Buck Owens, c. 1940.
Courtesy of Buck Owens Private Foundation.

Below: Left to right: Mary Lee Bounds,
Andy Bounds, Carl Lee, Buck Owens, c. 1941.
Courtesy of Buck Owens Private Foundation.

46

Bakersfield Bound

Top: Bill Woods & His Orange Blossom Playboys, early 1950s. Left to right: Buck Owens, Dick Wheeler, Johnny Cuviello, Bill Woods, Lawrence Williams. *Courtesy of Buck Owens Private Foundation.*

Above: Buck and Bonnie Owens, c. 1948. *Courtesy of Buddy Alan Owens and Michael Owens.*

One night at a local roller-skating rink, Owens met an aspiring singer named Bonnie Campbell. "I fell in love with her the first time I saw her," he said. The teenagers married on January 13, 1948; had two sons, Buddy and Michael; and then separated after three years together. By this time, most everyone in Buck's family who had made the trip from Texas to Arizona had moved on to Bakersfield. Not long after Buck and Bonnie split up, Bonnie, Buddy, and Michael made the trek to Bakersfield as well, initially moving in with Buck's Uncle Vernon, Aunt Lucille, and cousin Jimmy.

When Buck finally moved to Bakersfield in May of 1951 to be near his family, he immediately joined the town's raucous music scene. First he became a guitarist in Dusty Rhodes's band, at a club called the Roundup. In short order, Owens moved on to Bill Woods's group, the Orange Blossom Playboys. Woods was known for having the best musicians in town in his band, and he ruled the roost at Bakersfield's hottest joint, the Blackboard Cafe.

Although Buck would eventually become one of the most noted singers in country music history, he spent his earliest days onstage in Bakersfield playing guitar—specifically, a used, early model Fender Telecaster he'd bought for $35 from Lewis Talley, a Bakersfield singer, songwriter, and musical entrepreneur. Through Woods's connections with various recording artists based on the West Coast, Owens worked occasional sessions in Los Angeles.

On September 8, 1953, Owens was lead guitarist on a recording session by Leonard Sipes—a singer known professionally as Tommy Collins. The session resulted in Collins's first and biggest hit: "You Better Not Do That." Released in January 1954, it rose to #2 during its twenty-one week stay on *Billboard*'s country charts. Collins's producer, Capitol Records' Ken Nelson, was impressed enough with Buck's playing to call on him frequently over the next several years.

Lawrence "Piano" Junior "Steel Guitar"

Buck "Guitar"

Ray "Drums"

Buck Owens AND HIS SCHOOLHOUSE PLAYBOYS

Buck Owens & His Schoolhouse Playboys, c. 1956. Left to right: Owens, Lawrence Williams, Junior Stonebarger, Ray Heath. *Courtesy of Buck Owens Private Foundation.*

Recording Artist

During his tenure as a member of Bill Woods's Orange Blossom Playboys, Owens became the band's lead singer, in addition to his ongoing guitar duties. When Woods decided to leave the Blackboard in March 1955, Buck Owens & His Schoolhouse Playboys took over on the bandstand.

In August of that year, Owens cut four songs as a solo artist, using a Los Angeles studio. His first two singles were released on Claude Caviness's Pep Records, but with scant distribution, they went nowhere. Despite these low sales figures, Caviness wanted more, so Owens recorded two songs at a small Bakersfield studio owned by Lewis Talley. Since rockabilly was the latest rage—thanks to Elvis Presley's skyrocketing career—Owens wrote and recorded two up-tempo songs, "Hot Dog" and "Rhythm and Booze." But before the single was released, he got cold feet about stepping away from the country music he was known for around Bakersfield. To protect the musical identity he'd established, he told Caviness he wanted to use the pseudonym Corky Jones. In retrospect, Owens needn't have worried: The "Corky Jones" single made no more noise than his previous Pep releases.

There would be one last Pep single, "There Goes My Love" backed with "Sweethearts in Heaven." Although this release also tanked, Buck's "There Goes My Love" became a #15 hit for country star George Morgan in 1957, providing Owens with his first chart-making record as a songwriter.

Left: Buck Owens had a hand in writing all four songs recorded by the Farmer Boys at their last session, in 1957. He also played guitar on the recordings, including "Someone to Love" (co-written by Joe "Red" Simpson).

Above right: Buck Owens with Cliffie Stone (center) and Ken Nelson at Capitol Studios, c. 1967.
Courtesy of Buck Owens Private Foundation.

Songwriter

In 1957, Buck continued his lengthy stand at the Blackboard while also working Capitol sessions for Ken Nelson. Capitol artists Bobby Adamson and Woody Wayne Murray—the Farmer Boys—arrived at Capitol's Los Angeles studios on February 21, 1957, prepared to record four songs Owens had written or co-written. Before the session got underway, Buck (who had once again been hired to play guitar) got some unexpected news from an angry Ken Nelson. Nelson had already sent the act the four songs he wanted them to record that day, but the Farmer Boys had decided they preferred Buck's compositions.

Nelson was livid—and not simply because approving songs was his prerogative: In addition, he typically used songs published by Central Songs, a company he owned with fellow Capitol producers Cliffie Stone and Lee Gilette. Worried that he might lose his lucrative Capitol session work, Owens quickly explained that the Farmer Boys had come to his house asking for songs, and that he had no idea Nelson had already chosen the material for that day's session. When Nelson heard the quality of Buck's originals, he acquiesced (though he claimed two of the compositions for Central Songs and the other two for Beechwood Music, a Capitol affiliate). Realizing for the first time that Owens was not only a strong singer and instrumentalist but also a talented songwriter, the producer had a recording contract ready for Buck's signature by the time the Farmer Boys' session was over.

Buck Owens & the Bar-K Gang, with guest Loretta Lynn on the *Bar-K Jamboree* TV program, c. 1959. Left to right: Rollie Webster, Don Markham (behind Don Rich), Rich, Barbara Vogel (also behind Rich), Gail Harris, Harvie Johnson, Loretta Lynn, Buck Owens, Dusty Rhodes (behind Owens).

One of Don Rich's fiddles, made in Germany in 1936 by Oskar Meinel. *Courtesy of Vance and Vic Ulrich. Photo by Bob Delavante.*

The Capitol Years Begin

With Nelson producing, Owens recorded four songs at his first solo Capitol session on August 30, 1957. His debut single, released in October, didn't excite radio programmers, and six months later his second single suffered the same fate. In truth, Nelson had failed to capture on tape the raw excitement that made Buck's Blackboard performances such a draw.

During the six months between his first two Capitol singles, Owens revealed his entrepreneurial side. Despite his steady gig at the Blackboard, he left to pursue a business opportunity in Puyallup, Washington, a Tacoma suburb. Here he acquired an interest in radio station KAYE. While in Washington, he worked at the station as a disc jockey and ad salesman. Owens also formed a band called the Bar-K Gang and hosted a local television show called the *Bar-K Jamboree* on KTNT in Tacoma. The band featured a sixteen-year-old fiddle player named Donald Eugene Ulrich, whom Buck would rechristen as Don Rich.

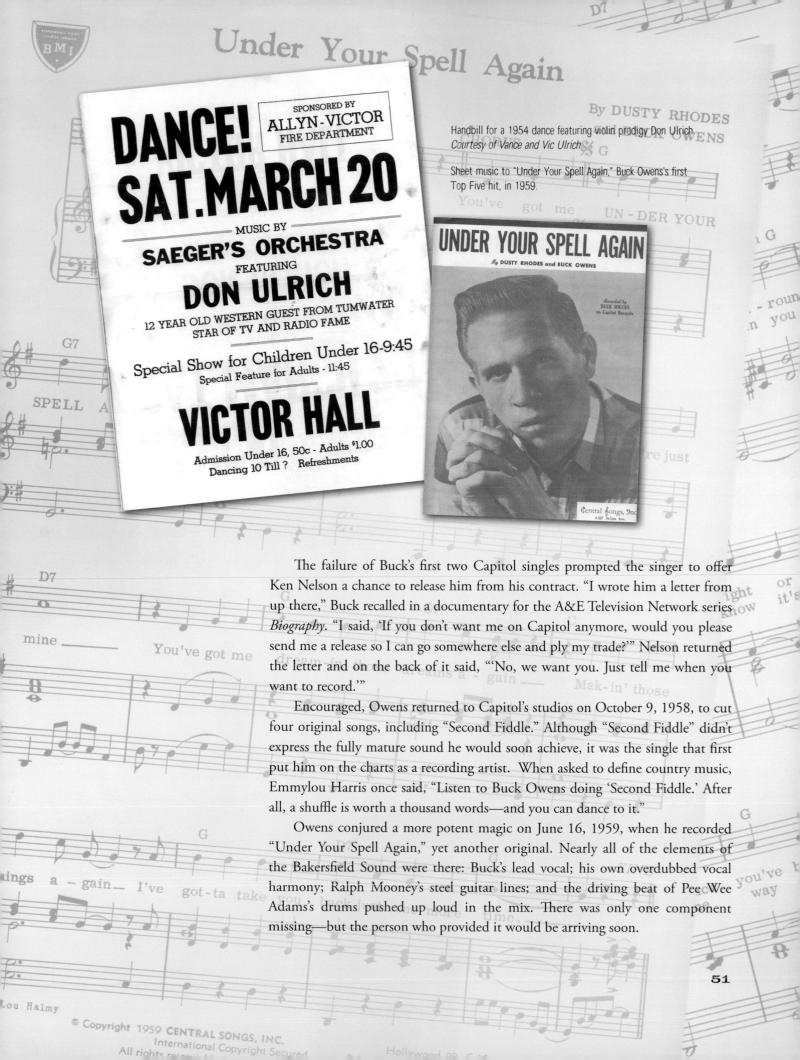

DANCE!
SAT. MARCH 20

SPONSORED BY
ALLYN-VICTOR
FIRE DEPARTMENT

MUSIC BY
SAEGER'S ORCHESTRA
FEATURING
DON ULRICH
12 YEAR OLD WESTERN GUEST FROM TUMWATER
STAR OF TV AND RADIO FAME

Special Show for Children Under 16-9:45
Special Feature for Adults - 11:45

VICTOR HALL

Admission Under 16, 50c - Adults $1.00
Dancing 10 Till ?   Refreshments

Handbill for a 1954 dance featuring violin prodigy Don Ulrich.
Courtesy of Vance and Vic Ulrich.

Sheet music to "Under Your Spell Again," Buck Owens's first
Top Five hit, in 1959.

UNDER YOUR SPELL AGAIN
By DUSTY RHODES and BUCK OWENS

Recorded by
BUCK OWENS
on Capitol Records

Central Songs, Inc.

The failure of Buck's first two Capitol singles prompted the singer to offer Ken Nelson a chance to release him from his contract. "I wrote him a letter from up there," Buck recalled in a documentary for the A&E Television Network series *Biography*. "I said, 'If you don't want me on Capitol anymore, would you please send me a release so I can go somewhere else and ply my trade?'" Nelson returned the letter and on the back of it said, "'No, we want you. Just tell me when you want to record.'"

Encouraged, Owens returned to Capitol's studios on October 9, 1958, to cut four original songs, including "Second Fiddle." Although "Second Fiddle" didn't express the fully mature sound he would soon achieve, it was the single that first put him on the charts as a recording artist. When asked to define country music, Emmylou Harris once said, "Listen to Buck Owens doing 'Second Fiddle.' After all, a shuffle is worth a thousand words—and you can dance to it."

Owens conjured a more potent magic on June 16, 1959, when he recorded "Under Your Spell Again," yet another original. Nearly all of the elements of the Bakersfield Sound were there: Buck's lead vocal; his own overdubbed vocal harmony; Ralph Mooney's steel guitar lines; and the driving beat of PeeWee Adams's drums pushed up loud in the mix. There was only one component missing—but the person who provided it would be arriving soon.

51

Back to Bakersfield

In June 1960—after having Top Five hits the previous year with "Under Your Spell Again" and his follow-up, "Above and Beyond"—Owens sold his Washington business interests and prepared to return to Bakersfield. "I asked Don Rich if he wanted to come with me," Owens explained, "but he said his folks were set on him going to college. We shook hands and I thought, 'Well, that's probably the last time I'll see him.' After I'd been back in Bakersfield about four months I get this letter from Don, written on notebook paper in pencil. It said, 'Dear Chief, I don't like this college stuff. It ain't going to work out for me. I've decided I want to make music my life. In the months that you've been gone I've been playing with lots of other people, but they don't do it the way I like it. I like it the way we did it when you were here, so if you have a job for me, I'd like to come to work for you.'

"In the letter," Owens continued, "when he asked me for a job, he spelled it 'J-O-B-B.' At the end of the letter he wrote, 'I got to go get that damn cat out of the kitchen or Mama's going to kill me when she comes in.' He had spelled cat 'C-A-T-T,' so it was easy for me to see that Don Rich wasn't going to have much of a college career. I decided I'd better give him a job."

Rich moved to Bakersfield in November 1960, and the two musicians began touring together, capitalizing on Buck's hit singles and using whatever musicians were available in the clubs and honky-tonks they worked. Buck helped Don develop his guitar skills, and by the time they hit the road, both were playing Fender Telecasters, creating a unique country sound.

Along with their masterful guitar work, their vocal harmonies were downright unworldly. "It was almost like Don and I were joined together at the hip," Owens said. "Our singing was so much alike—the tones, the attack of the voices was almost exact. It seemed as if he could read my mind." Before long, Buck added a drummer, a steel guitarist, and a bass player to his Buckaroos—so named by one of the group's early bass guitarists, Merle Haggard. The musical framework for the Owens-Rich vocal team was now complete.

In contrast to many country bandleaders, Owens closely controlled his recording sessions and used the same musicians in the studio and on the road. As a result, his releases had a fresh, exciting "live" feel. In addition, his songs featured catchy hook lines and melodies. Unlike elaborate Nashville Sound productions filled with string sections and background vocal groups, his tight, five-piece band showcased incisive electric guitar parts, tasteful steel guitar solos and fills, and a steady beat, all undergirding Owens and Rich's high, perfectly matched harmony. Though grounded in honky-tonk tradition, Owens's music was decidedly new. His flashy costumes and fast-paced, high-energy shows made it seem revolutionary.

(continued on page 56)

Right: Buck Owens and Don Rich with pickup musicians, including Fred Maddox on bass, 1961.

Below: Made by Nudie's Rodeo Tailors in the early 1960s, this jacket is part of the first Nudie suit owned by Buck Owens. *Courtesy of Buck Owens' Crystal Palace. Photo by Bob Delavante.*

Below right: Don Rich's leather jacket, with fringe and animal hide, worn onstage in the early 1960s. *Courtesy of Vance and Vic Ulrich. Photo by Bob Delavante.*

AUG 1961

RED SIMPSON

Many country fans remember Red Simpson for blacktop-themed hits such as "Roll, Truck, Roll," "The Highway Patrol," and "I'm a Truck." But Simpson, who moved with his family to a migrant labor camp near Bakersfield in 1937, wasn't a truck driver at all: He was a multi-talented songwriter and musician whom Bob Dylan called "one of the architects of the Bakersfield Sound."

Known as the Bard of Bakersfield, Simpson penned more than forty songs for Buck Owens and Merle Haggard, including "Gonna Have Love," "Sam's Place," "Kansas City Song," "Close Up the Honky Tonks," and "You Don't Have Very Far to Go." Owens praised him as "one of the most prolific songwriters . . . that I ever met." Over the years, dozens of artists, including Johnny Paycheck, the Byrds, Lucinda Williams, Alan Jackson, and Dwight Yoakam, have recorded Simpson originals.

Red's older brother Buster was one of the earliest members of Bill Woods's Orange Blossom Playboys, and Red grew up around Bakersfield's dance halls. When Buster died at an early age, Woods took Red under his wing. "We used to sit down in his living room and write songs," Simpson explained. "That's the way I kind of got started writing." Soon Woods and Owens were calling Red to cover for them on guitar when they needed a break from their nightly gig at the Blackboard. Fuzzy Owen hired him to play piano full time at the Clover Club, and in 1957 Simpson made his first record on the Tally label, established by Owen and Lewis Talley.

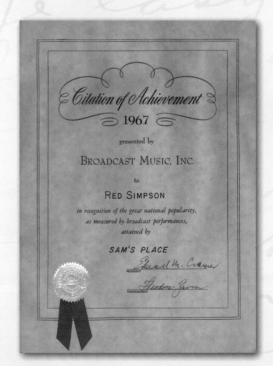

Left: Red Simpson was nicknamed "Suitcase Simpson" because he carried manuscripts of original songs he was pitching in this metal case. Red acquired it during the Korean War, when he was stationed on the hospital ship SS *Repose. Courtesy of Red Simpson.*
Photo by Bob Delevante.

Above: BMI citation presented to Red Simpson, who co-wrote Buck Owens's 1967 smash hit "Sam's Place" with Owens. *Courtesy of Red Simpson.*

Above left: Red Simpson and several of his navy shipmates performed as the Repose Ramblers, pictured here at the Orphan's Home in Inchon, Korea, in 1953. Left to right: Pappy Reed, "Little," Tommy Moss, "Barnett," Arlen Babcock, Red Simpson. *Courtesy of Red Simpson.*

Above right: Red Simpson, c. 1966.

When Buck Owens began recording his compositions in the early 1960s, Simpson signed a writing contract with Central Songs, a music publishing firm owned by Cliffie Stone and Capitol producers Ken Nelson and Lee Gillette. When Nelson was looking for an artist to record an album of trucking songs, Stone recommended Simpson. By 1966, he was touring with Owens, and that year *Roll, Truck, Roll* reached #4 on *Billboard's* country album chart. Simpson's rich baritone voice, combined with Gene Moles's lean, twisting guitar leads and Leo LeBlanc's rolling pedal steel, made his 1960s Capitol recordings some of the finest examples of the Bakersfield Sound.

Simpson had his biggest hit in 1972 when "I'm a Truck" became a #4 country single. He continued to write and record, but gave up touring in 1984 as trucking songs fell out of vogue. He settled into his role as an elder statesman of the Bakersfield Sound, and his records are still prized by fans of trucking music and West Coast twang.

—*Scott B. Bomar*

I'M A BUCK OWENS TIGER

Top: Buck Owens & the Buckaroos onstage, c. 1966. Left to right: Doyle Holly, Don Rich, Owens, Willie Cantu (barely visible behind Owens), Tom Brumley.
Courtesy of Buck Owens Private Foundation.

Above: Promotional bumper sticker, marketed by Buck Owens Enterprises in the 1960s.
Courtesy of Buck Owens Private Foundation.

Left: Buck Owens's 1964 Fender Telecaster with custom silver-sparkle finish, used at countless performances, including his 1966 Carnegie Hall concert.
Courtesy of Buck Owens' Crystal Palace. Photo by Bob Delavante.

(from page 52)

Glory Years

In the world of country music, the 1960s belonged to Buck Owens. Between March 1960 and November 1969, his singles charted no fewer than forty-four times. His first #1 hit was 1963's "Act Naturally," followed by "Love's Gonna Live Here," which topped *Billboard*'s country singles chart for an astounding sixteen weeks.

Next came the two-sided 1964 hit "My Heart Skips a Beat" backed with "Together Again," the latter song an Owens composition that would be recorded by artists including Glen Campbell, Ray Charles, Jerry Lee Lewis, Dean Martin, Emmylou Harris, and Gram Parsons.

By mid-decade, Owens was one of America's busiest performers. In 1966 alone he notched three more

Above: Dean Martin and Buck Owens, late 1960s.
Courtesy of Buck Owens Private Foundation.

Top right: Buck Owens in the KUZZ van, late 1960s.
Courtesy of Buck Owens Private Foundation.

Right: Picture sleeve for "Only You (Can Break My Heart)," Buck Owens's eighth #1 hit (1965). Left to right: Doyle Holly, Tom Brumley, Willie Cantu, Owens, Don Rich.

#1 singles; released four albums; created his own half-hour syndicated television program, *The Buck Owens Ranch Show*; appeared on national TV shows hosted by Jimmy Dean, Dean Martin, and Jackie Gleason; bought radio station KUZZ in Bakersfield (part of what would become a multi-state broadcasting empire); and staged a sold-out show at Carnegie Hall. The Carnegie Hall concert was released as a live album (which also went to #1) and featured what has come to be known as the classic Buckaroos lineup, which lasted from 1963–67: Don Rich on lead guitar, fiddle, and harmony vocals; Tom Brumley on pedal steel; Doyle Holly on bass; and Willie Cantu on drums. Meanwhile, Owens continued to develop his Blue Book music publishing company and, with his manager, Jack McFadden, a booking agency and management firm.

Buck's other #1 hits during the 1960s included "I've Got a Tiger by the Tail," the instrumental "Buckaroo," "Think of Me," "Open Up Your Heart," "I Don't Care (Just as Long as You Love Me)," "Waitin' in Your Welfare Line," and "Tall Dark Stranger." All told, thirty-three Owens singles cracked the country Top Ten in a single decade. No one else came close.

But judging by the awards handed out by the Nashville-based Country Music Association (CMA), the country establishment didn't yet appreciate Owens's accomplishments. With the exception of two Instrumental Group of the Year awards honoring the Buckaroos in 1967 and 1968, it was as if Buck Owens didn't exist. The chasm between Bakersfield and Nashville was as wide as the distance between the two cities.

Buck Owens on the set of *Hee Haw*, c. 1969. Left to right: Jim Hager, Susan Raye, Owens, Gunilla Hutton, Jon Hager, Doyle Holly. *Courtesy of Buck Owens Private Foundation and Capitol/EMI.*

Right: Buck Owens American model guitar, marketed by Sears, Roebuck and Co., beginning in the late 1960s. *Photo by Bob Delavante.*

Far Right: Buck Owens's handwritten notes, prepared for the eulogy he delivered at Don Rich's funeral. *Courtesy of Vance and Vic Ulrich..*

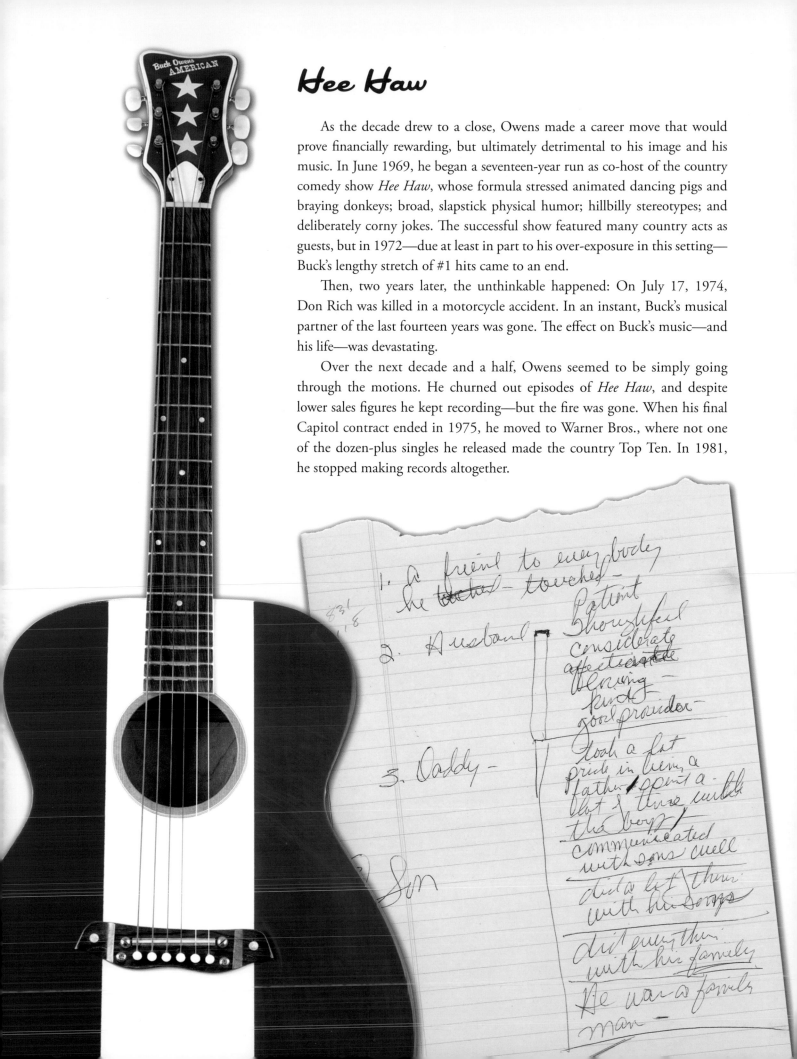

Hee Haw

As the decade drew to a close, Owens made a career move that would prove financially rewarding, but ultimately detrimental to his image and his music. In June 1969, he began a seventeen-year run as co-host of the country comedy show *Hee Haw*, whose formula stressed animated dancing pigs and braying donkeys; broad, slapstick physical humor; hillbilly stereotypes; and deliberately corny jokes. The successful show featured many country acts as guests, but in 1972—due at least in part to his over-exposure in this setting—Buck's lengthy stretch of #1 hits came to an end.

Then, two years later, the unthinkable happened: On July 17, 1974, Don Rich was killed in a motorcycle accident. In an instant, Buck's musical partner of the last fourteen years was gone. The effect on Buck's music—and his life—was devastating.

Over the next decade and a half, Owens seemed to be simply going through the motions. He churned out episodes of *Hee Haw*, and despite lower sales figures he kept recording—but the fire was gone. When his final Capitol contract ended in 1975, he moved to Warner Bros., where not one of the dozen-plus singles he released made the country Top Ten. In 1981, he stopped making records altogether.

Comeback

In 1986, Dwight Yoakam released his first LP. That album, *Guitars, Cadillacs, Etc., Etc.*, was a paean to the Bakersfield Sound Owens was so pivotal in creating. The following year, Yoakam released *Hillbilly Deluxe*, an album containing the Owens-influenced hit "Little Ways." On September 23, 1987, Dwight paid a visit to Buck's Bakersfield office and convinced his idol to join him onstage that night at the Kern County Fair. Soon they appeared together on a national television special, performing a song Buck had recorded years earlier: "Streets of Bakersfield." In April 1988, Yoakam and Owens recorded the song and later watched the single scale the country charts. "Streets of Bakersfield" became Buck's twenty-first #1 single.

For the first time in years, the momentum was in Buck's favor. When Capitol executive Jim Foglesong asked Owens to return to the roster, he agreed to sign a new contract with his old label.

On November 16, 1988, Capitol released *Hot Dog!* Produced by Buckaroos keyboard player Jim Shaw, the solo album was Buck's first in eleven years. More than three decades had passed since he recorded the single "Hot Dog" for Pep Records—back in the days when he considered it too close to rock & roll to release under his own name.

The new album put Owens in the public eye again—not as the co-host of a hillbilly-based TV show, but as a recording artist and a major concert attraction. It was only natural that his touring partner would be his staunchest supporter: Dwight Yoakam.

Dwight Yoakam onstage with Buck Owens and the Buckaroos, c. 1988. Left to right: Yoakam, Doyle Singer, Owens.
Courtesy of Buck Owens Private Foundation.

Next, Buck decided to re-record "Act Naturally," one of his biggest hits, with former Beatle Ringo Starr, whose band had a hit with their version of the song in 1965. The Owens-Starr rendition of "Act Naturally," title track for a 1989 Owens album, remained on the charts for almost three months. The single received a CMA nomination for Vocal Event of the Year and a Grammy nomination for Best Country Vocal Collaboration.

Owens had accomplished a great deal, but more was still to come. In October 1996, he presided over the opening of Bakersfield's Crystal Palace, a combination museum and dinner club that was all the things a former Bakersfield nightspot like the Blackboard was not—spacious, beautifully appointed, and comfortable for performers and audiences alike. Located on a street that would ultimately be named Buck Owens Boulevard, the venue was an instant success.

That same year, Buck Owens was finally inducted into the Country Music Hall of Fame. Most of his best-known contemporaries, including George Jones, Johnny Cash, Marty Robbins, and Roger Miller, had already received the honor. So had Buck's one-time bass player, Merle Haggard, and former *Hee Haw* cast members Minnie Pearl and Grandpa Jones. For most of his life, Owens had fought Nashville's way of making music and doing business, but his contributions to country music couldn't be ignored any longer.

Above: Custom-made leather guitar strap, presented to Buck Owens by Brad Paisley. *Courtesy of Buck Owens' Crystal Palace. Photo by Bob Delavante.*

Top Left: Buck Owens and Ringo Starr at London's Abbey Road Studios in 1989, recording "Act Naturally" as a duet. *Courtesy of Buck Owens Private Foundation.*

Top Right: Buck Owens presenting one of his red, white, and blue Fender Telecasters to Bob Dylan in 2005, while Dylan was touring with Merle Haggard. Left to right: Dylan, Haggard, Owens. *Courtesy of Buck Owens Private Foundation.*

Right: Acclaimed Tex-Mex musician Flaco Jimenez used this Hohner Corona II accordion on Buck Owens and Dwight Yoakam's recording of "Streets of Bakersfield." *Courtesy of Buck Owens' Crystal Palace. Photo by Bob Delavante.*

Showman to the End

When the new millennium began, Buck Owens and Dwight Yoakam ushered it in together at the Crystal Palace. But soon thereafter, Buck's health began to deteriorate. He maintained a steady schedule of Palace performances with the Buckaroos every weekend until suffering a mild stroke in February 2004. Even though he resumed working with the band a few months later, there were nights when he didn't feel well enough to play. Friday, March 24, 2006, was one of those nights.

As Owens walked through the parking lot on the way to his car, a couple excitedly told him they had traveled more than seven hundred miles to see him perform. A showman to the end, he went back inside the Palace, strapped on his guitar, and stayed on the bandstand for an hour and a half.

A few hours later, on March 25, Owens suffered cardiac arrest and passed away at his ranch north of town.

Buck Owens's influence reached from Bakersfield, California, around the world—across generations of fans and musicians. His original songs and distinctive recordings, both vital to the music of Bakersfield, have inspired not only country stars from Merle Haggard to Dwight Yoakam, Marty Stuart, and Brad Paisley, but also R&B singers such as Ray Charles and rock acts including the Beatles, the Byrds, the Flying Burrito Brothers, the Eagles, and even the Grateful Dead. His artistic independence and business achievements set a powerful example for performers in many fields, and his innovative musical approach stands as a beacon for others. Buck Owens always followed his own path, and in doing so he became a country music icon. ■

Far Left: Buck Owens, 1999. *Courtesy of Buck Owens Private Foundation. Photo by Felix Adams.*

Left: Bolero jacket, with embroidery and rhinestones, made by Manuel and worn by Buck Owens in the latter part of his career. *Courtesy of Buck Owens' Crystal Palace. Photo by Bob Delavante.*

Early 1970s Fender Telecaster Limited Edition model with red, white, and blue sparkle finish; Buck Owens's name inlaid on the fretboard; and gold-plated hardware. *Courtesy of Buck Owens' Crystal Palace. Photo by Bob Delavante.*

BONNIE OWENS

Bonnie Owens never had a Top Ten hit, but she was a central figure in Bakersfield country music. At various times, her personal and professional lives became intertwined with those of Buck Owens, Merle Haggard, and key Bakersfield Sound architect Fuzzy Owen.

Born in Blanchard, Oklahoma, on October 1, 1929, Bonnie Maureen Campbell joined the Dust Bowl migration when her family moved to Arizona. Inspired by yodeling cowgirl Patsy Montana, Campbell set her sights on a singing career while still a young girl. When she was fifteen, in 1945, Bonnie met Buck Owens at a Mesa, Arizona, roller rink, and they married three years later.

Bonnie and Buck were separated by the time they arrived in Bakersfield in 1951. They divorced two years later, but remained friends. A single mother, Bonnie worked as a car-hop and a cocktail waitress to support her young sons. She was also a gifted vocalist and budding songwriter. Bonnie became known as the "singing waitress" because she often took breaks from serving drinks to sing with the band at the Blackboard and the Clover Club.

Owens achieved her greatest success as duet partner and backup singer with her second husband, Merle Haggard. The Academy of Country Music named her Female Vocalist of the Year in 1965. With Haggard she won the ACM award for Vocal Duet of the Year from 1965 to 1968.

—*Museum Staff*

Opposite page:
Bonnie Campbell in the 1940s.

Bonnie Owens's manuscript for "I'm a Lucky Woman," typed on stationery from Shade Tree Music, the publishing company owned by Merle Haggard. *Courtesy of Michael Owens.*

Bonnie Owens, c. 1965. *Courtesy of Buddy Alan Owens.*

Above: Bonnie Owens with her sons, Michael Owens and Buddy Alan Owens. *Courtesy of Buddy Alan Owens.*

Right: Bonnie, Red Simpson, Don Rich, and Buck Owens, 1963. *Courtesy of Michael Owens.*

MERLE
HAGGARD

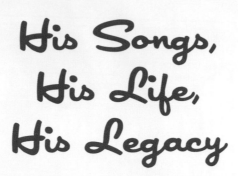

His Songs, His Life, His Legacy

By Robert Price

Merle Haggard's career has been parsed for political meaning and influence since he thrust himself into the national consciousness in 1969—and swung outside the insular orbit of late-1960s country music.

That, of course, was the year Haggard came out with "Okie from Muskogee," the song he has never escaped, despite indications, as the years passed, that he might wish he could. Though he never said so in exactly these terms, "Okie" was bigger, deeper, and more complicated than he ever imagined it could be. The Bakersfield-born singer-songwriter got an inkling of its power the night he first performed it at a club for noncommissioned Army officers at Fort Bragg, North Carolina, in mid-1969: The men rioted, but in a good way—the way a soldier riots when he's overcome with pride and relief and joy at the realization that this thing, this malignancy that had been building up in his soul, has a name, and that by celebrating patriotism and traditional values despite a growing anti-establishment counterculture, these words ease the agony. That realization was so intoxicating it seized some of the nation's most ambitious business and political figures: Conservative leaders could see that the white, working-class angst depicted in the song's plain-spoken lyric lit a path to greater power.

And so began the courtship of Merle Haggard. During the presidential campaign of 1972, Alabama Governor George Wallace, the political personification of blue-collar malaise, asked for his endorsement. Ernest Tubb and Marty Robbins had already signed on. Haggard, by then understanding the vein of resentment he'd unintentionally tapped, declined. President Richard Nixon sought his favor, and in 1972 conservative icon Ronald Reagan, then governor of California, granted Haggard a pardon for the crimes of his youth.

But Haggard, at his core, was not political, not in the traditional sense. Over the years he has made conflicting comments on "Okie," some investing the song with deep meaning, others virtually dismissing it as a whim of the moment. With remarkable consistency, however, he has spun poems from his pain and weaved stories around his burdens, both inherited and self-inflicted. And when, amidst the Vietnam War, he was confronted with black-and-white images of rage and violence on college campuses across America, he saw only class warfare—the long-haired privileged class vs. the plain-living underclass. His underclass. It stirred an anger in him, the same quiet anger that had tormented him for almost as long as he could remember. It wasn't the national argument over military intervention in a faraway land that stoked the fightin' side of Haggard. It was his differentness as an Okie, and his pride in that differentness.

Top: Merle Haggard cradles the armload of Country Music Association awards he won in 1970. *Courtesy of Buddy Alan and Michael Owens.*

Below: As governor of California in 1972, Ronald Reagan granted Merle Haggard a full pardon for his crimes.

Top: Merle Haggard's home in Oildale, California.

Below: Merle, at age seven, with his father, James, and dog, Jack. *Courtesy of Lillian Haggard.*

Bottom: A teenaged Merle Haggard in the 1950s. *Courtesy of Lillian Haggard.*

From Rambler to Rake-Hell

Johnny Cash's life story went celluloid in 2005 with the acclaimed *Walk the Line*, but the screenplay of Haggard's tortured and charmed life would seem to have more potential. The child of working-class, pre–Dust Bowl Okie migrants, he was born in Bakersfield in 1937 and raised in a modest, 1,000 square-foot home in Oildale that his father fashioned from a surplus Southern Pacific boxcar. Merle was devastated at age nine by the sudden, unexpected death of his father from a brain hemorrhage. He hopped his first freight train at eleven, got his first guitar at twelve, and, during a hitchiking foray, lost his virginity to an Amarillo prostitute at fourteen. He spent most of his fifteenth year in juvenile detention centers, including two stints at Ione, California's Preston School of Industry, a high-security lockup that made a permanent dent in his psyche.

At sixteen, Haggard met and played for his idol, Lefty Frizzell, whose music would leave a lasting imprint on the younger singer. Impressed by their chance backstage encounter at Bakersfield's all-ages Rainbow Gardens dance hall, the star put him onstage as his opening act. At seventeen Haggard married a waitress, Leona Hobbs, and they soon had a child. At eighteen, he began serving nineteen months in the Ventura County jail for car theft. At nineteen, having established himself as something of a commodity at Bakersfield clubs including the Blackboard Cafe, the Clover Club, and the Lucky Spot, Haggard made a guest appearance on KBAK-TV's *Chuck Wagon Gang*, a local show starring Billy Mize and Cliff Crofford. Mize told him afterward he could go far if he kept his head on straight. That, sadly, was then too much to ask of the young performer.

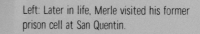

Left: Later in life, Merle visited his former prison cell at San Quentin.

Right: Merle Haggard (center) with son Marty and mother, Flossie, 1960s.

San Quentin

When Haggard was twenty, he bungled a burglary of a diner he and his accomplices erroneously believed had closed for the night. When the incredulous owner confronted them, the Haggard gang ran, even though the owner knew them all by name. Haggard was arrested, escaped from jail, and was arrested again. Kern County Sheriff's Deputy Tommy Gallon finally nabbed him at his brother Lowell's house on Christmas Eve (but won Haggard's everlasting respect by allowing him to finish his highball before handcuffing him).

In court a few days later, defense attorney Ralph McKnight asked for leniency—if only for the sake of Haggard's poor, long-suffering mother. "This mother has tried very hard," McKnight told the judge, presumably nodding deferentially toward Flossie Haggard, seated somewhere in the gallery. The Honorable Norman F. Main was unmoved. "If he had tried half as hard as his mother did," the judge began in his preamble to the eventual sentence: prison.

Haggard deprived both men of the partial songwriting credit they arguably deserved for "Mama Tried."

That crime alone wasn't what put Haggard in San Quentin; it was merely the last straw, the icing on a seven-year run of delinquency, drunkenness, theft, assault, and escape. There would be no escape from the most feared state penitentiary in California.

The most defining two years and nine months of Haggard's life began on March 26, 1958—the day he became Prisoner A-45200. During his stay as a guest of California taxpayers, Haggard and his fellow inmates stomped, hooted, and hollered their way through a concert by Johnny Cash, then a rising star on America's music scene. Haggard and Cash later recalled the concert on August 2, 1969, when viewers witnessed Haggard's guest appearance on ABC-TV's *The Johnny Cash Show*.

"It's funny you mention that, Johnny," Haggard said.

"What?"

"San Quentin."

"Why's that?"

"The first time I ever saw you perform, it was at San Quentin."

"I don't remember your being on that show, Merle."

"I was in the audience, Johnny."

To those who knew him mostly for his tender odes to poor, ever-striving families and pugilistic anthems of red-blooded patriotism, this was another layer of Merle Haggard. Prior to the broadcast, his criminal past was no secret, but Cash had urged him to share this part of his life on network television. Now, more clearly than ever, a national audience understood that Haggard originals like "Branded Man" were far from fictional. However the media and his publicists spun his reformed-but-misunderstood hoodlum persona, it was entirely authentic—and, in retrospect, may have been the most genuine of his songs' various narrators.

Just as he sang in "Mama Tried," Haggard indeed "turned twenty-one in prison," although his fifteen-year sentence didn't quite rise to the level of "doin' life without parole." Nevertheless, incarceration didn't take right away, and Haggard suffered the consequences: Guards caught him drunk on home brew, and he wound up in solitary confinement. He spent his twenty-first birthday in a nine-by-twelve, cement-floored box with only a pair of pajama bottoms, a Bible, and a blanket. Those seven days were life changing—not because of isolation per se, but because he shared that isolation with San Quentin's death row inmates, whose voices he could hear through a vented plumbing alley. Among them was convicted robber-rapist-kidnapper Caryl Chessman, the notorious "Red-Light Bandit." Chessman won several stays of execution, but on May 2, 1960, having apparently run out of chances, he was led into the gas chamber. As the poisonous vapor enveloped him, the phone rang. Too late, it was a judge's secretary with news of yet another stay.

A New Start

Those events left Haggard chastened by a somber realization: Opportunity doesn't just knock, it phones as well, and sometimes to no avail. Haggard asked for a more challenging job in the prison textile mill, worked toward his high school equivalency degree, and joined the prison band. The parole board was suitably impressed, and on November 3, 1960, prison officials gave him $15 and a bus ticket back to Bakersfield. Haggard had spent seven of his twenty-three years in reform schools or in a cell.

He took a job digging ditches for his brother Lowell's electrical company while looking for work in Bakersfield's many nightclubs and honky-tonks. Within weeks, he found a fill-in job at the Lucky Spot playing with fiddler Jelly Sanders, whose quintet covered for Johnny Barnett's house band twice a week. There Haggard met Charles "Fuzzy" Owen and Lewis Talley, cousins from Arkansas who'd been developing their own record label. In Haggard, they realized they might have found an artist. "He was paranoid, just got out of the joint," Owen said. "But he was good. Even his mistakes sounded good. I thought, 'Hey, I better listen to this guy a little bit.'"

Bill Rea, who was married to Haggard's sister, Lillian, decided to help. Cousin Herb Henson's *Trading Post*, a five-day-a-week Bakersfield TV show, featured national and regional country stars, but Henson, the program's genial, piano-playing host and ad pitchman, regularly brought in relative unknowns as well. "Usually one night a week we had somebody local—you know, try to give somebody a chance no one had heard of," said Al Brumley Jr. (brother of Buck Owens steel player Tom Brumley), who performed on the show himself and lined up guest talent. "I got this call one day: 'I'd like you to listen to my brother-in-law.' So I said, 'Sure, bring him down.' In walks this shy, quiet fella. I had my old Martin guitar leaned up in the corner. I said, 'Pick that up and do me one.' I can't be sure, but I think it was a Lefty Frizzell song, 'Always Late.' Herb put him on the show five nights a week."

Left: Fuzzy Owen (left) and Merle Haggard, early 1960s.

Right: left to right: Lewis Talley, Dallas Frazier, and Merle Haggard. BMI Awards, 1973. *Courtesy of Dallas Frazier.*

Haggard's star rose quickly over the next three years. He went into the old Quonset hut his friends Owen and Talley called a recording studio and, using their borrowed tape machine and a three-channel mixing console, recorded "Skid Row" and "Singing My Heart Out." The plan was to sell Haggard's Tally Records catalog, such as it was, to a major record label. "Merle's basically a shy guy, he's not a pusher," Brumley said. "Fuzzy really got it done for him. But he had a hard time selling him to anybody. Fuzzy would play him and these record guys would say, 'I don't hear anything.' That's your college graduates for you."

Capitol A&R man Ken Nelson knew better than that, but he was taking his sweet time. So, while Nelson was waffling about adding yet another name to Capitol's substantial roster of Bakersfield talent, Haggard traveled to Las Vegas on a whim and wound up playing bass in Wynn Stewart's band. Haggard's weekly salary, $225, was the highest he'd ever made in any legitimate job. More valuable was the friendship he forged with Stewart. Haggard gambled away more money than he earned, but before he left Las Vegas he persuaded Stewart to allow him to record a Stewart original, "Sing a Sad Song." Haggard put it to vinyl in 1963, and in January 1964 it climbed to #19 on *Billboard's* country charts.

Above: Merle Haggard and Bonnie Owens with their children and friends at home in Oildale, California, 1966. Left to right: Kelly Haggard, Bonnie Owens, Noel Haggard, Michael Owens, (unidentified), Merle Haggard, Buddy Alan Owens, Fuzzy Owen, Dana Haggard. *Courtesy of Michael Owens.*

Left: Merle Haggard and Bonnie Owens photo shoot for their 1966 album, *Just Between the Two of Us. Courtesy of Buddy Alan Owens.*

By this time Haggard had formed a reliable band, with Fuzzy on steel, Lewis on guitar, and Fuzzy's girlfriend, Bonnie Owens, on backing vocals. Although many of Haggard's songs had a sublimely reassuring simplicity, nothing in his personal or professional life was ever simple. Bonnie was one memorable example: She had been married to Buck Owens, a longtime club and session guitarist who by now was on the cusp of superstardom. That had been years before, however; now Bonnie was a regular on Herb Henson's *Trading Post* and a Clover Club cocktail waitress who sometimes took a turn at the microphone or paused mid-shift to scribble song-lyric fragments onto cocktail napkins as inspiration struck. Within four years, to Fuzzy's shock and dismay, she would be Mrs. Merle Haggard. Nevertheless, his friendship and professional relationship with Merle endured.

In mid-1964, while Haggard's band was playing a show near Sacramento, Bonnie introduced him to songwriter Liz Anderson. Initially reluctant to sit still long enough to listen to any of her songs, Haggard was floored by "Just Between the Two of Us" and "(My Friends Are Gonna Be) Strangers." Both became hits for him on Tally Records, and the latter gave his band a name—the Strangers. The two songs—along with Haggard's hard-edged vocals and apparent sales potential—won over Ken Nelson, and in April 1965, with Fuzzy's blessing and encouragement, Haggard signed with Capitol.

(continued on page 78)

Three-piece suit with rhinestones and embroidery, made by Nudie's Rodeo Tailors and worn by Merle Haggard in the 1970s.

FUZZY OWEN AND LEWIS TALLEY

As pioneers of Bakersfield's club scene and recording industry, Charles "Fuzzy" Owen and Lewis Talley were significant players in making the city an important music center of the 1950s and beyond. In the late 1940s Fuzzy Owen moved to Bakersfield from Arkansas, where he had played steel guitar on Little Rock's *Barnyard Frolic*, broadcast over radio station KRLA. Once in town, he teamed with his cousin Lewis Talley, whose near-perfect imitations of Hank Williams and Ernest Tubb made him a local favorite. The two began working Bakersfield clubs and became fixtures of the local country music community by the early 1950s. "If someone had told me when I was about sixteen years old that I would ever be as big a star as Lewis Talley, I would have laughed," Merle Haggard later reflected.

Both Talley and Owen recorded for the local Mar-Vel label, established by enterprising country singer Hillbilly Barton, like them a recent arrival in Bakersfield. One of Mar-Vel's releases was a Barton original that Fuzzy recorded with then-girlfriend Bonnie Owens, called "A Dear John Letter." "I figured the song was a hit," Talley explained, "and I traded a 1947 Kaiser for it." He then sold a half-interest in the copyright to Owen for $150.

Below: left to right, Fuzzy Owen, Merle Haggard, and Lewis Talley in the studio, 1960s.

Released on Tally Records in 1963, Merle Haggard's first chart hit was produced by Fuzzy Owen..

Lewis Talley   *Radio Show Early 1950's*

Above left: 1950s newspaper advertisement for Fuzzy Owen & the Sun Valley Playboys' residency at Bakersfield's Clover Club. The band included Bonnie Owens and Lewis Talley. *Courtesy of Fuzzy Owen.*

Above right: Lewis Talley and Fuzzy Owen. *Courtesy of Fuzzy Owen.*

In the meantime, Ferlin Husky was getting a strong response to the record on his Bakersfield radio show on KBIS and suggested that Capitol producer Ken Nelson record it at an upcoming Jean Shepard session. Shepard's recording, which featured recitations by Husky, and named Owen and Talley as writers, went to #1 and became the first major country hit to emerge from Bakersfield.

In 1955 Lewis Talley opened a recording studio, and Fuzzy soon joined him as a partner in Tally Records with an eye toward the burgeoning rockabilly field. In addition to their own discs, they released singles by artists including Cliff Crofford, George Rich, Harlan Howard, Herb Henson, and Red Simpson, whose first recording appeared on the label. Owen and Talley spent the next several years performing in clubs and traveling to Hollywood to play on Capitol sessions. In 1963 the Tally label broke through when Bonnie Owens's rendition of "Why Don't Daddy Live Here Anymore" (credited to Fuzzy Owen and up-and-coming songwriter Dallas Frazier) reached #25 on *Billboard*'s country chart.

In 1963 Tally signed Merle Haggard to an artist contract. By mid-decade Fuzzy had sold Bonnie and Merle's masters to Capitol, and he and Talley became permanent members of Haggard's business organization.

—*Scott B. Bomar*

(from page 74)

Hitmaker

Between 1963 and 1989 Haggard placed 101 recordings in *Billboard*'s country charts. Of these, seventy-one reached the Top Ten, with thirty-eight rising to #1. In the studio, he built this impressive catalog with a fairly consistent group of Bakersfield-based musicians, augmented by talented players like Billy Mize, Glen Campbell, and James Burton, the consummate studio gunslinger who appeared on most of Haggard's recordings between 1967 and 1972 and also worked closely with Elvis Presley from 1969 until Presley's death in 1977. "[Haggard] called me up and told me he wanted me for something he was working on," said Burton years later. "He'd heard a song that I'd recorded with Ricky Nelson called 'You Just Can't Quit.' He says, 'Man, I'm writing a song that [needs] that sound, that guitar.' Can't remember what the song was now, or even if we recorded it, but we found some other things to do."

"The Bottle Let Me Down" (1966) was Haggard's first studio collaboration with Burton. Others included "Mama Tried" (1968), on which Burton's Dobro memorably played off Roy Nichols's Fender Telecaster; "I Take a Lot of Pride in What I Am" (1968); and Burton's two Haggard favorites, "Workin' Man Blues" (1969) and "Sing Me Back Home" (1967), on which he contributed uncredited guitar work.

Guitarist Roy Nichols, who'd made a name for himself as a teenage prodigy for the Maddox Brothers & Rose long before joining the Strangers, took Haggard's show on the road. Nichols played his own parts and Burton's, too, having intently watched his studio bandmate lay down distinctive licks even when Nichols himself wasn't in the lineup for a particular session.

Far Left: Merle Haggard and Bonnie Owens with the
Strangers, c. 1966. Standing left to right: Eddie Burris,
Fuzzy Owen, Jerry Ward, George French, and Roy Nichols.

Above: Merle Haggard in the studio, 1960s.

Right: Roy Nichols used this Regal resonator guitar
while a member of Merle Haggard's band, the Strangers.
Courtesy of Marty Stuart.

The Bakersfield Sound

By 1972, Haggard and Buck Owens were clearly the chief purveyors of the Bakersfield Sound, the West Coast brand of country music that prompted someone—perhaps a music writer or record-label exec—to bestow the appellation "Nashville West" on the gritty farm and oil town one hundred miles north of Los Angeles. In truth, the music coming out of Bakersfield honky-tonks, and out of Capitol Records, was in no way a single "sound." Although his Dust Bowl credentials were every bit as valid as Haggard's, and he perfected his style before Haggard did, Owens's version of the Bakersfield Sound was markedly different. His lyrics were generally simple and straightforward, conveying a single, unadulterated emotion. Likewise, his recordings were typically driving and treble-heavy, his rockabilly, blues, and Tex-Mex influences readily apparent.

By contrast, Haggard often penned complex, multi-dimensional lyrics built around poetic images, as in "Mama's Hungry Eyes." And while he drew from bluesy balladeers Jimmie Rodgers and Lefty Frizzell, Haggard looked primarily to western swing, the music of Milton Brown, Spade Cooley, and the man he revered most, Bob Wills, who had moved to the West Coast in 1943. Haggard's bandmates, including Roy Nichols and steel players Norm Hamlet and Ralph Mooney breathed that same air.

The stew of influences that made Haggard who he was, musically and otherwise, changed flavor over time. "Picasso was known for being part of a certain period in art and culture, and that's the case with Merle, too," said singer-songwriter Marty Stuart in 2011. "He was exposed to a certain special time in American music, and it stayed with him. Merle was like a sponge. Whether it was ballad music, or blues, or Mexican, he was soaking it up. Then, when he came out with *A Tribute to the Best Damn Fiddle Player in the World* [Haggard's 1970 album honoring Wills], it was like a line in the dirt, and from that point on, you could always hear that influence." Haggard learned to play fiddle and brought in six members of the Texas Playboys for the project, recorded in his home studio not far from Bakersfield.

Haggard's subtle jazz inflections actually started a little earlier, certainly by the time "I Started Loving You Again" appeared on his 1968 album *The Legend of Bonnie and Clyde*. Many of his recordings have a similar lilt, and as his career progressed, it became more pronounced. The lightness, even delicacy, of Haggard's clear, twang-free voice, even when he was singing about his "fightin' side," only accentuated his debt to jazz. To be sure, he believed he had fused jazz and country. "I realized that jazz meant that you could play anything," said Haggard in 2000, the only country musician who has appeared on the cover of *DownBeat*, the jazz-music bible. "It meant that you were a full-fledged musician, that you could play with Louis Armstrong or Johnny Cash." As Stuart averred, Haggard removed all doubt about his affection for "country jazz" and its chief pioneer with his Wills tribute.

Above: Merle Haggard, c. 1985.

Left: Merle Haggard with Bob Wills, 1971.

Left background: Merle Haggard's handwritten lyrics to his enduring ballad "I Started Loving You Again." *Courtesy of Marty Stuart.*

Oilfield Laureate

From a commercial standpoint, Haggard's career had by 1990 gone largely the way many fifty-year-old performers' careers tend to go. He bounced from label to label, embittered by perceived (and, without a doubt, accurately portrayed) indifference on the part of people who were supposed to be promoting him. But his songwriting never stopped; in fact it barely slowed, and critics continued to acknowledge its undiminished quality.

In 1999, feeling unappreciated and forgotten, Haggard sold his Kern River mansion and moved to Lake Shasta, 450 miles north of the city he'd always called home. As he wrote on the last page of his second autobiography, 1999's *Merle Haggard's My House of Memories* (with Tom Carter), he didn't expect to come back. Today, he shares a 200-acre spread, Shade Tree Manor, with fifth wife Theresa Lane. The couple has raised two children. He has a full-scale recording studio, adorned with assorted artifacts: dusty, half-empty bourbon bottles abandoned by Lewis Talley; one of Bob Wills's old cigar butts, tenderly preserved under glass; and framed words of inspiration imparted by Roger Miller: "We Shall Over Dub."

But Haggard couldn't stay away from Bakersfield, or from nearby Oildale, where he did much of his youthful damage. He returns to play two or three times a year at Bakersfield's Fox Theater or the Crystal Palace, the dinner club opened in 1996 by Buck Owens. Directions to the club: From Fresno, proceed south on Highway 99 five miles past the Merle Haggard Drive off-ramp to Buck Owens Boulevard. Exit and look for the building that's least like the others.

In many ways Haggard's political outlook remains as ambiguous as it was four decades ago. He wrote a song for Hillary Clinton, perhaps in hopes she'd use it in her 2008 political campaign, and he has expressed both exasperation with and admiration for Barack Obama. The snapshot in time known as "Okie from Muskogee" is no longer the defiant anthem it once seemed, and some fans view it as a comedic relic of an earlier era. Yet given today's economic woes and continuing class warfare, it may well resonate with working class Americans of the twenty-first century. For whatever reason, audiences still ask for "Okie"—demand it, in fact. Haggard obliges them, and probably always will.

Haggard's story of redemption could well be the story of his hometown, a blue collar city of humble origins. Like Haggard, Bakersfield has always seen itself as an entity apart, an island of

(continued on page 86)

MOSRITE

In the 1960s, the Bakersfield area was home to several guitar manufacturers, including Gruggett, Hallmark, and Mosrite. The most successful company, Mosrite of California, was started in 1959 by brothers Andy and Semie Moseley, who moved to Bakersfield from Oklahoma when they were children.

At the peak of production, in 1968, Mosrite made more than a thousand guitars a month, including double- and triple-neck models. Mosrites have been favored by a wide range of guitarists, including country virtuoso Joe Maphis, surf-music favorites the Ventures, and punk-rocker Johnny Ramone of the Ramones.

Bakersfield session guitarist, sideman, and recording artist Gene Moles explained the Mosrite appeal: "It was a well-designed instrument. It felt good to a guitar player when he grabbed it. It had a narrow neck and a low profile, so you didn't have to push down as hard on the strings to play it."

—*Museum Staff*

Left: 1960s advertisement for Mosrite electric guitars. *Courtesy of Deke Dickerson.*

Below: Barbara Mandrell's first record, "Queen for a Day," was released in 1966 on Mosrite Records.

Above: Semie Moseley with a Mosrite Joe Maphis Doubleneck model guitar.

Left: Prototype of Semie Moseley's Buckaroo model electric guitar, made for Don Rich of Buck Owens and the Buckaroos. *Photo by Bob Delevante.*

"COUSIN HERB" AND BAKERSFIELD COUNTRY MUSIC TELEVISION

Bakersfield's raucous honky-tonk scene of the 1950s and '60s had civilized opening acts well suited for family consumption. The hour or so immediately following the local evening news was devoted to country music. Led by a cadre of easygoing hosts, the competing live programs featured some of country's biggest stars, sprinkled with local heroes and low-profile guests.

Best known was chatty, amiable "Cousin Herb" Henson, whose forty-five-minute *Trading Post* show lasted more than ten years, a period that virtually spanned the Eisenhower and Kennedy administrations.

As legend goes—and the story of his arrival and all-too-short reign qualifies as legend—Henson, an itinerant musician from East St. Louis, jumped off a Union Pacific boxcar somewhere on the outskirts of Bakersfield one day in 1946. Seven years later, having made a name for himself as a salesman as much as a piano-plinking entertainer, Henson pitched the idea of a daily television show to the general manager of KERO-TV. Henson closed the deal, and *Cousin Herb's Trading Post* debuted in September 1953. Regular cast members included Fuzzy Owen, Lewis Talley, Bonnie Owens, and the man who had invited Henson to come to town in the first place, an Arvin, California, preacher's son and World War II shipyard worker named Bill Woods.

Left: *The Jimmy Thomason Show*, 1953.
Left to right: Thomason, Gene Moles, Cliff Crofford, Johnny Barnett. *Courtesy of Eugene Moles Jr.*

Below: Autographed signboard used on Bill Woods's TV program on Bakersfield channel 29. *Courtesy of Thomas Sims Archives.*

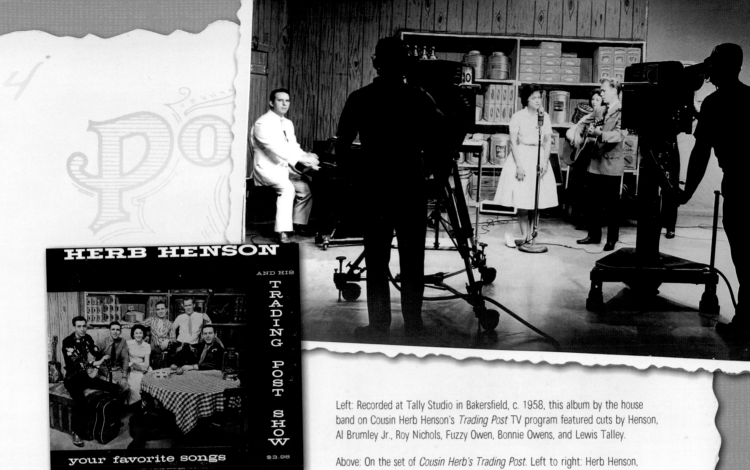

Left: Recorded at Tally Studio in Bakersfield, c. 1958, this album by the house band on Cousin Herb Henson's *Trading Post* TV program featured cuts by Henson, Al Brumley Jr., Roy Nichols, Fuzzy Owen, Bonnie Owens, and Lewis Talley.

Above: On the set of *Cousin Herb's Trading Post*. Left to right: Herb Henson, Bonnie Owens, Rose Lee Maphis, Al Brumley Jr. *Courtesy of Billy Mize.*

Henson had some good company on Central Valley television screens. His primary competition was Texan Jimmy Thomason, a Waco-born fiddler who, with his wife, co-hosted *The Louise and Jimmy Thomason Show*. They had launched their program on KAFY-TV (later known as KBAK-TV) just a few weeks before Henson's debut. Both shows were instant hits.

There were also Billy Mize, a steel guitarist with matinee-idol looks; his cohort Cliff Crofford, who teamed with Mize to bring *The Chuck Wagon Gang* to Bakersfield audiences; and Dave Stogner, another Texas fiddler, who brought front-porch charm from Fresno south to Bakersfield via *The Dave Stogner Show*.

Along the way, Bakersfield television hosts launched a number of performers' careers and cultivated an audience for the country music variety programs of the decade that would follow—two, notably, involving one of Bakersfield's most famous country music performers. Buck Owens, who went on to star on *Buck Owens' Ranch* and *Hee Haw*, perfected his TV smile on Bakersfield's airwaves.

Although local country-music TV shows lasted well into the 1960s, Bakersfield country telecasting lost much of its magic on November 26, 1963, when Henson died of a heart attack. News broadcasts had been full of grief and speculation for four days at that point, ever since the assassination of President John F. Kennedy. And then this—the music man of Bakersfield television, dead at thirty-eight.

Said Al Brumley Jr., producer of *Cousin Herb's Trading Post*: "It was like losing the president all over again."

—*Robert Price*

Top: Merle Haggard and fellow award recipients at the Kennedy Center Honors gala, Washington, D.C., 2010. Standing, left to right: Haggard, Bill T. Jones, and Paul McCartney. Seated: Jerry Herman and Oprah Winfrey. Photo by Ron Sachs-Pool.

(from page 81)

stubborn independence. Literally, Bakersfield is one hundred miles from cities of comparable size. Culturally, economically, and politically, however, it's a thousand figurative miles outside socially progressive California. The state's prevailing character has evolved over the years, often in contradictory fashion, but the maverick nature of its booming petroleum capital has remained steadfast. Though the people of Bakersfield didn't always appreciate what they had in Haggard, at times some of them surely recognized the spirit of their city in his poetry.

At seventy-five, Haggard remains a product of his upbringing—rough around the edges, a little bit hacked off, and unwaveringly proud of who he is, how he got here, and who brought him. His pride in the dignity and essential goodness of the displaced underclass from which he sprang is reciprocal: Haggard shaped Bakersfield, too. "He's given that place an integrity-based identity," Stuart said. "I know how it is in Bakersfield; it's not exactly Hollywood and glamour. I'm from Mississippi, and the thing we hear all the time is that we're at the top of all the wrong lists and at the bottom of all the good lists. That's an issue that those two places share. But Merle gives Bakersfield that integrity, that special character, and it's because he's speaking truth, and speaking it in the words of the common man. He's not a ditty act."

No, Merle Haggard is not a ditty act. He's America's oilfield laureate, a truck-stop philosopher with dirty fingernails and a clear, open channel between his heart, his head, and his voice. He would not have been the same without Bakersfield. Bakersfield most certainly would not have been the same without Merle Haggard. ∎

BILLY MIZE

Only two hours away, Los Angeles was where Bakersfield's country stars went to make records, buy stage clothes, and appear on syndicated television programs. Hollywood tailors Nudie Cohn and Nathan Turk outfitted Buck Owens and others in colorful and flashy couture, while Capitol's Ken Nelson oversaw the recording of dozens of hits by Bakersfield artists in the label's Hollywood studio.

The symbiotic relationship between Bakersfield and Los Angeles was epitomized by Billy Mize. The handsome singer, songwriter, and steel guitarist got his start in 1953 as a co-star on the Bakersfield TV show *Cousin Herb's Trading Post*. Through his frequent appearances on *Town Hall Party* and other Los Angeles TV programs beginning in the 1950s, Mize built a fan base in that urban market.

In the mid-1960s, Mize put countless miles on his Cadillac, driving back and forth between Bakersfield and Los Angeles five days a week to host two daily country music TV programs: Gene Autry's nationally syndicated *Melody Ranch* and the *Trading Post*, which he continued to helm after Henson passed away.

Mize received the Academy of Country Music's Personality of the Year award every year between 1965 and 1967. He recorded for Columbia, United Artists, and other labels, while enjoying success as a writer of hits for Marty Robbins, Charlie Walker, and other artists.

—*Museum Staff*

Below: Marty Robbins (left) and Billy Mize on a pilot episode of the *Billy Mize Music Hall*, taped in 1972. *Courtesy of Billy Mize and family.*

Right: In the mid-1950s, Cliff Crofford (left) and Billy Mize hosted the *Chuck Wagon Gang*, a country music TV program on Bakersfield station KBAK. The duo recorded several singles for Challenge Records and other labels. *Courtesy of Billy Mize and family.*

5858 SUNSET BOULEVARD • P.O. BOX 710 • LOS ANGELES, CALIFORNIA 90078

March 7, 1994

Dear Billy,

I was so happy to learn that you are having a special
tribute party in your honor. You are most deserving
of this special occasion.

A lot of years have passed since you hosted "Melody Ranch"
but I will never forget your talent, your great showmanship
and our friendship.

Although I cannot be with you for this celebration, I join
with your many friends in saluting you. You have my very
best wishes always.

Warmest personal regards,

Gene Autry

Mr. Billy Mize
c/o Ms. Neomia Cash
3716 Harmony Drive
Bakersfield, CA 93306

Above: Billy Mize, Pacoima, California, 1980s.
Courtesy of Billy Mize and family.

Right: A 1994 tribute concert in Bakersfield, honoring Billy Mize,
prompted this letter from singing cowboy legend Gene Autry.
The concert included performances by Merle Haggard, Buck
Owens, and Bonnie Owens. *Courtesy of Billy Mize and family.*

Left: Billy Mize's family, in Kern County, c. 1937, soon
after moving to California from Kansas. Left to right: Lelia
(mother), Raymond (father), Buddy (on Raymond's lap),
Billy, and June. *Courtesy of Billy Mize.*

SOURCES

DIM LIGHTS, THICK SMOKE, AND LOUD, LOUD MUSIC:
The Story of the Bakersfield Sound by Scott B. Bomar

BOOKS

Bull, Debby. *Hillbilly Hollywood: The Origins of Country & Western Style*. New York: Rizzoli International, 2000.

Dawidoff, Nicholas. *In the Country of Country: A Journey to the Roots of American Music*. New York: Random House, 1997.

Gregory, James N. *American Exodus: The Dust Bowl Migration and Okie Culture in California*. New York: Oxford University Press, 1999.

Grissim, John. *Country Music: White Man's Blues*. New York: Coronet, 1970.

Haggard, Merle, with Tom Carter. *Merle Haggard's My House of Memories: For the Record*. New York: HarperCollins, 2002.

Haggard, Merle, with Peggy Russell. *Sing Me Back Home: My Story*. New York: Simon and Schuster, 1983.

Haslam, Gerald W., with Alexandra Haslam Russell and Richard Chon. *Workin' Man Blues: Country Music in California*. Berkeley: University of California Press, 1999.

Hemphill, Paul. *The Nashville Sound: Bright Lights and Country Music*. New York: Simon and Schuster, 1970.

La Chapelle, Peter. *Proud to Be an Okie: Cultural Politics, Country Music, and Migration to Southern California*. Berkeley: University of California Press, 2007.

Mize, Sharon, ed. *Bakersfield Sound*. Bakersfield: Bakersfield Country, 1999.

ARTICLES

"Bakersfield Hosts Country Musicians." *The Bakersfield Californian*, April 27, 1972.

Briggs, Ed. "Country Music Capitol of the West." *Billboard: The World of Country Music 1966–1967*, 30–32.

Grossi, Mark. "A Sound Born in Bakersfield." *The Bakersfield Californian*, August 10, 1981.

Hunter, Glenn. "The Bakersfield Sound." *Westways*, July 1979, 28–32.

Kleiner, Richard. "Bakersfield Makes Its Own Kind of Music." *Sundowner*, July, 1973, 20–22.

Martin, Bryce. "Homegrown Bakersfield Music Survives Phases." *The Bakersfield Californian*, May 25, 1984.

McPeters, Buddy. "Junior Barnard: Hard Driving Soloist of Western Swing." *Guitar Player*, September 1983, 44, 47, 49.

Mitchell, Rick. "The Bakersfield Sound: Roots & Revivial." *Musician*, July 1989, 52–56, 58, 60, 62, 118.

Price, Robert. "Lights! Camera! Country! Bakersfield Bandstand." *Journal of Country Music* 23: 1 (2002): 18–24, 26.

Tittl, Pete. "When Every Corner Had a Guitar Player." *The Bakersfield Californian*, September 11, 1982.

Yaw, Ralph. "Cross Country Jamboree, Bakersfield, Cal." *Country and Western Jamboree*, August 1955, 12.

AUTHOR'S INTERVIEWS

Adams, Kay: August 13, 2009.

Anderson, Liz: January 20, 2006.

Barton, Billy: September 17, 2007.

Breeden, Gene: August 11, 2007; August 21, 2010.

Brumley, Tom: April 4, 2008.

Brumley, Al Jr: August 7, 2009.

Crofford, Cliff: December 4, 2006.

Cuviello, Johnny: March 17, 2008.

Durham, Bobby: November 17, 2005.

Frazier, Dallas: August 25, 2006; September 3, 2011.

Haggard, Merle: August 17, 2010.

Hamlet, Norm: December 5, 2005.

Hays, Tommy: December 5, 2005.

Holly, Doyle: January 25, 2006.

Howard, Jan: September 14, 2005; September 4, 2011.

Husky, Ferlin: October 17, 2006.

Mandrell, Barbara: September 21, 2006.

Maphis, Rose Lee: April 9, 2005.

Markham, Don: August 22, 2009.

Mize, Billy: November 19, 2005.

Mize, Buddy: January 19, 2006; February 20, 2011.

Moseley, Andy: September 24, 2006.

Nelson, Ken; October 3, 2005.

Owen, Fuzzy: July 24, 2007; May 11, 2011.

Paxton, Gary S.: August 13, 2009.

Payne, Dennis: August 5, 2006; January 25, 2011.

Shepard, Jean: October 23, 2006.

Simpson, Red: November 15, 2005; January 28, 2008;
    February 13, 2011; February 21, 2011.

Thomason, Louise: October 10, 2008.

Whittington, Oscar: February 2, 2007; July 26, 2007.

Wiggins, Susan Raye and Jerry: April 27, 2008.

Don Maddox of Maddox Brothers & Rose wore these boots, made by L. White Boot & Saddle Company of Fort Worth, Texas. *Courtesy of Marty Stuart. Photo by Bob Delevante.*

OTHER INTERVIEWS

Owens, Buck: Videotaped interview by David Alan, 1989.

Owens, Buck, and Merle Haggard: Videotaped interview by
    Storme Warren for *TNN Country News*, June 16, 1995.

Woods, Bill: Videotaped interview by Glenn J. Pogatchnik,
    August 6, 1998.

LINER NOTES

Bomar, Scott B. Notes to Red Simpson, *Hello, I'm Red Simpson*. Bear Family BCD 16944 (2012).
Escott, Colin. Notes to Wynn Stewart, *Wishful Thinking*. Bear Family BCD 15886 (2000).
Ginell, Cary. Notes to The Farmer Boys, *Flash Crash and Thunder*. Bear Family BCD 15579 (1991).
Skinker, Chris. Notes to Jean Shepard, *The Melody Ranch Girl*. Bear Family BCD 15905 (1996).
Vinicur, Dale. Notes to Tommy Collins, *Leonard*. Bear Family BCD 15577 (1992).

RADIO

Voices from the Dust Bowl. Lost and Found Sound Series, National Public Radio. *All Things Considered*,
    July 28, 2000.

VIDEO

Bakersfield Country! Directed by Paula Mazur. KCET–Los Angeles, November 15, 1991.
Billy Mize & The Bakersfield Sound. Directed by William J. Saunders. Old City Entertainment, March 19, 2012.
Lost Highway: The Story of Country Music. Produced by William Naylor. BBC, 2003.
Merle Haggard: Learning to Live with Myself. Directed by Gandulf Hening. American Masters Series, PBS, July 21, 2010.
Workin' Man Blues. KVIE Public Television, Sacramento, California. ViewFinder Series #401, July 12–19, 2006.

FROM THE BACK ROADS OF TEXAS TO THE STREETS OF BAKERSFIELD

The Musical Journey of Buck Owens by Randy Poe

BOOKS

Burke, Kathryn. *The Dust Bowl, the Bakersfield Sound, and Buck.* North Charleston, SC: BookSurge Publishers, 2007.

Haslam, Gerald W., with Alexandra Haslam Russell and Richard Chon. *Workin' Man Blues: Country Music in California.* Berkeley: University of California Press, 1999.

Kingsbury, Paul, ed. *The Encyclopedia of Country Music.* New York: Oxford University Press, 1998.

Nelson, Ken. *My First 90 Years Plus 3.* Pittsburgh: Dorrance Publishing Co., Inc., 2007.

ARTICLES

Price, Robert. "Doing It His Way Until the End," *The Bakersfield Californian*, March 26, 2006.

LINER NOTES

Dickinson, Chris. Notes to Buck Owens, *Young Buck: The Complete Pre-Capitol Recordings of Buck Owens.* Audium 8124 (2001).

Owens, Buck. Notes to Don Rich & the Buckaroos, *Country Pickin': The Don Rich Anthology.* Sundazed SC 11091 (2000).

AUTHOR'S INTERVIEWS

Cantu, Willie: June 2009.

Shaw, Jim: April 2009.

OTHER INTERVIEWS

Owens, Buck: self-interviews, 2000–2005.

VIDEO

Buck Owens—Acting Naturally. A&E Home Video, 2001.

Right: Nathan Turk made matching stage costumes with *Grapes of Wrath*-themed embroidery for the Maddox Brothers & Rose. This suit was worn by bass player Fred Maddox. *Photo by Bob Delevante*

MERLE HAGGARD
His Songs, His Life, His Legacy by Robert Price

BOOKS
Gregory, James N. *American Exodus: the Dust Bowl Migration and Okie Culture in California.*
New York: Oxford University Press, 1998.

Haggard, Merle, with Tom Carter. *Merle Haggard's My House of Memories: For the Record.*
New York: HarperCollins, 2002.

Haggard, Merle, with Peggy Russell. *Sing Me Back Home: My Story.* New York: Times Books, 1981.

Haslam, Gerald, W., with Alexandra Haslam Russell and Richard Chon. *Workin' Man Blues: Country
Music in California.* Berkeley: University of California Press, 1999.

La Chapelle, Peter. *Proud to Be an Okie: Cultural Politics, Country Music, and Migration to Southern
California.* Berkeley: University of California Press, 2007.

ARTICLES
Halberstadt, Alex. "Brilliant Careers: Sound and Vison: Merle Haggard." Salon.com, November 14,
2000.

"Merle Haggard Offers Proof of His High Spirits by Telling 5,095 Texans, 'This Round's on Me.'" *People*,
February 7, 1983. Retrieved from www.people.com/people/archive/article/0,,20084217,00.html.

Price, Robert. "The Bakersfield Sound: Raw, Real, and Not Nashville." *The Bakersfield Californian*, June 22, 1997.

LINER NOTES
Price, Robert. Notes to Merle Haggard, *The Original Outlaw.*
Time-Life Records/EMI Music Special Markets/Sony BMG
Music Entertainment Custom Marketing Group
M19506 = 09463–92092–2–4 = A710531 (2007).

Vinicur, Dale. Notes to Merle Haggard, *Untamed Hawk:
The Early Recordings of Merle Haggard.* Bear Family Records
BCD 15744 (1995).

AUTHOR'S INTERVIEWS
Brumley, Al Jr.: November 7, 2011.

Burton, James: November 11, 2011.

Stuart, Marty: November 18, 2011.

*The Academy of Country Music's 1969 Song of the Year award
for Merle Haggard's "Okie from Muskogee," published by Buck
Owens's Blue Book Music. Courtesy of Buck Owens' Crystal Palace.
Photo by Bob Delevante.*

SUGGESTED BOOKS, RECORDINGS, AND DVDS

Books and Articles

Boyd, Jean A. *The Jazz of the Southwest: An Oral History of Western Swing.* Austin: University of Texas Press, 1998.

Gregory, James N. *American Exodus: The Dust Bowl Migration and Okie Culture in California.* New York: Oxford University Press, 1999.

Haslam, Gerald W., with Alexandra Haslam Russell and Richard Chon. *Workin' Man Blues: Country Music in California.* Berkeley: University of California Press, 1999.

Kienzle, Rich. *Southwest Shuffle: Pioneers of Honky-Tonk, Western Swing, and Country Jazz.* New York: Routledge, 2003.

La Chapelle, Peter. *Proud to Be an Okie: Cultural Politics, Country Music, and Migration to Southern California.* Berkeley: University of California Press, 2007.

McNutt, Randy. *Guitar Towns: A Journey to the Crossroads of Rock 'n' Roll.* Bloomington: Indiana University Press, 2002.

Nickell, Jeff, and Sarah Woodman. *Hard Drivin' Country: The Honky Tonks, Musicians, and Legends of the Bakersfield Sound.* Bakersfield: Kern County Museum, 2009.

Price, Robert. "The Bakersfield Sound." *The Bakersfield Californian*: June 22, 1997; June 29, 1997; July 6, 1997.

Recordings

Adams, Kay. *Wheels & Tears.* Sundazed SC9002 (2004).

Burton, James, and Ralph Mooney. *Corn Pickin' and Slick Slidin'.* Sundazed 9009 (2005).

Collins, Tommy. *The Capitol Collection.* Koch / EMI Special Markets 9845 (2005).

_____. *Leonard.* Bear Family BCD 15577 (1992).

Cooley, Spade. *Spadella: The Essential Spade Cooley.* Sony / Legacy CK-57392 (1994).

Farmer Boys. *Flash Crash and Thunder.* Bear Family BCD 15579 (1993).

Gosdin Brothers. *Sounds of Goodbye.* Big Beat CDWIKD 235 (2003).

Haggard, Merle. *Down Every Road 1962–1994.* Capitol 7243-8-35712-2-2 (1996).

Haggard, Merle, & Bonnie Owens. *Just Between the Two of Us.* King KSCD-5119 (2000).

Husky, Ferlin. *Early Capitol Recordings 1953–1955.* British Archive of Country Music CD D 121 (2005).

Husky Ferlin, with Terry Preston and Simon Crum. *Echoes in My Heart: The Early Years.* Acrobat Music Group ACMCD 4320 (2004).

Maddox Brothers & Rose. *America's Most Colorful Hillbilly Band: Their Original Recordings 1946–1951.* Arhoolie CD 391 (1993).

Maphis, Joe, and Rose Lee. *Ridin' the Frets*. Jasmine Records 3590 (2010).

Owens, Bonnie. *Queen of the Coast*. Bear Family Records BCD 16178 (2007).

Owens, Buck. *The Buck Owens Collection (1959–1990)*. Rhino R2 71016 (1992).

_____. *Bound for Bakersfield 1953–1956: The Complete Pre-Capitol Collection*. Rockbeat B005DZMMBC (2011).

Owens, Buck, & His Buckaroos. *Carnegie Hall Concert*. Sundazed SC 11090 (2000).

Sanders, J.R. "Jelly." *Fiddlin' Around Bakersfield*. Jim and Jack Records 4653 (2011). Download only.

Shepard, Jean. *Honky-Tonk Heroine: Classic Capitol Recordings, 1952–1964*. Country Music Foundation CMF-021D (1995).

Simpson, Red. *Roll, Truck, Roll*. Sundazed SC 9003 (2004).

Stewart, Wynn. *Come On*. Bear Family BCD 17252AH (2011).

_____. *Wishful Thinking*. Bear Family BCD 15886 JI (2000).

Various Artists. *Bakersfield Rebels*. Ace CDWIKD232 (2004).

Various Artists. *Just Around Bakersfield: Rock Bop Country*. Classics 724 (2009).

Various Artists. *Road to Bakersfield*. IMC Music Ltd. / Country Stars CTS 55511 (2004).

Various Artists. *Swing West! Vol. 1: Bakersfield*. Razor & Tie 7930182197-2 (1999).

West, Speedy, and Jimmy Bryant. *Stratosphere Boogie: The Flaming Guitars of Speedy West and Jimmy Bryant*. Razor & Tie 82067 (1995).

Wills, Bob, & His Texas Playboys. Sony / Legacy 82796 93858 3 = CK 93859–CK 93862 (2006).

Woods, Bill. *Live at the Blackboard, Featuring Don Rich, Red Simpson, Don Markham and Fuzzy Owen*. The Titan Group TTG-1675 (1999).

DVDs

Billy Mize & the Bakersfield Sound. Dir. William J. Saunders. Old City Entertainment. March 19, 2012.

Buck Owens Ranch Show: #1 (March 15, 1966), #47 (March 27, 1967), and #158 (August 17, 1970). Available at www.buckowens.com.

Merle Haggard: Learning to Live with Myself. Dir. Gandulf Hening, American Masters Series. July 21, 2010. Available online at www.pbs.org/wnet/americanmasters/episodes/merle-haggard/watch-the-full-film/1605/.